SHORT WORKS OF THÉOPHILE GAUTIER

Copyright © 2008 BiblioBazaar
All rights reserved

Original copyright: 1908

SHORT WORKS OF THÉOPHILE GAUTIER

King Candaules, Clarimonde, and The Mummy's Foot

Translated by Lafcadio Hearn

SHORT WORKS OF
THÉOPHILE GAUTIER

CONTENTS

KING CANDAULES 9

CLARIMONDE 63

THE MUMMY'S FOOT 95

KING CANDAULES

CHAPTER I

Five hundred years before the Trojan war, and seventeen hundred and fifteen years before our own era, there was a grand festival at Sardes. King Candaules was going to marry. The people were affected with that sort of pleasurable interest and aimless emotion wherewith any royal event inspires the masses, even though it in no wise concerns them, and transpires in superior spheres of life which they can never hope to reach.

As soon as Phoebus-Apollo, standing in his quadriga, had gilded to saffron the summits of fertile Mount Tmolus with his rays, the good people of Sardes were all astir, going and coming, mounting or descending the marble stairways leading from the city to the waters of the Pactolus, that opulent river whose sands Midas filled with tiny sparks of gold when he bathed in its stream. One would have supposed that each one of these good citizens was himself about to marry, so solemn and important was the demeanour of all.

Men were gathering in groups in the Agora, upon the steps of the temples and along the porticoes. At every street corner one might have encountered women leading by the hand little children, whose uneven walk ill suited the maternal anxiety and impatience. Maidens were hastening to the fountains, all with urns gracefully balanced upon their heads, or sustained by their white arms as with natural handles, so as to procure early the necessary water provision for the household, and thus obtain leisure at the hour when the nuptial procession should pass. Washerwomen hastily folded the still damp tunics and chlamidæ, and piled them upon mule-wagons. Slaves turned the mill without any need of the overseer's whip to tickle their naked and scar-seamed shoulders. Sardes was hurrying itself to finish with those necessary everyday cares which no festival can wholly disregard.

The road along which the procession was to pass had been strewn with fine yellow sand. Brazen tripods, disposed along the way at regular intervals, sent up to heaven the odorous smoke of cinnamon and spikenard. These vapours, moreover, alone clouded the purity of the azure above. The clouds of a hymeneal day ought, indeed, to be formed only by the burning of perfumes. Myrtle and rose-laurel branches were strewn upon the ground, and from the walls of the palaces were suspended by little rings of bronze rich tapestries, whereon the needles of industrious captives—intermingling wool, silver, and gold—had represented various scenes in the history of the gods and heroes: Ixion embracing the cloud; Diana surprised in the bath by Actaeon; the shepherd Paris as judge in the contest of beauty held upon Mount Ida between Hera, the snowy-armed, Athena of the sea-green eyes, and Aphrodite, girded with her magic cestus; the old men of Troy rising to honour Helena as she passed through the Skaian gate, a subject taken from one of the poems of the blind man of Meles. Others exhibited in preference scenes taken from the life of Heracles, the Theban, through flattery to Candaules, himself a Heracleid, being descended from the hero through Alcaeus. Others contented themselves by decorating the entrances of their dwellings with garlands and wreaths in token of rejoicing.

Among the multitudes marshalled along the way from the royal house even as far as the gates of the city, through which the young queen would pass on her arrival, conversation naturally turned upon the beauty of the bride, whereof the renown had spread throughout all Asia; and upon the character of the bridegroom, who, although not altogether an eccentric, seemed nevertheless one not readily appreciated from the common standpoint of observation.

Nyssia, daughter of the Satrap Megabazus, was gifted with marvellous purity of feature and perfection of form; at least such was the rumour spread abroad by the female slaves who attended her, and a few female friends who had accompanied her to the bath; for no man could boast of knowing aught of Nyssia save the colour of her veil and the elegant folds that she involuntarily impressed upon the soft materials which robed her statuesque body.

The barbarians did not share the ideas of the Greeks in regard to modesty. While the youths of Achaia made no scruples of allowing their oil-anointed torsos to shine under the sun in the stadium, and while the Spartan virgins danced ungarmented before the altar of Diana, those of Persepolis, Ebactana, and Bactria, attaching more importance to chastity of the body than to chastity of mind, considered those liberties allowed to the pleasure of the eyes by Greek manner as impure and highly reprehensible, and held no woman virtuous who permitted men to obtain a glimpse of more than the tip of her foot in walking, as it slightly deranged the discreet folds of a long tunic.

Despite all this mystery, or rather, perhaps, by very reason of this mystery, the fame of Nyssia had not been slow to spread throughout all Lydia, and become popular there to such a degree that it had reached even Candaules, although kings are ordinarily the most illy informed people in their kingdoms, and live like the gods in a kind of cloud which conceals from them the knowledge of terrestrial things.

The Eupatridæ of Sardes, who hoped that the young king might, perchance, choose a wife from their family, the hetairæ of Athens, of Samos, of Miletus and of Cyprus, the beautiful slaves from the banks of the Indus, the blond girls brought at a vast expense from the depths of the Cimmerian fogs, were heedful never to utter in the presence of Candaules, whether within hearing or beyond hearing, a single word which bore any relation to Nyssia. The bravest, in a question of beauty, recoil before the prospect of a contest in which they can anticipate being outrivalled.

And nevertheless no person in Sardes, or even in Lydia, had beheld this redoubtable adversary, no person save one solitary being, who from the time of that encounter had kept his lips as firmly closed upon the subject as though Harpocrates, the god of silence, had sealed them with his finger, and that was Gyges, chief of the guards of Candaules. One day Gyges, his mind filled with various projects and vague ambitions, had been wandering among the Bactrian hills, whither his master had sent him upon an important and secret mission. He was dreaming of the intoxication of omnipotence, of treading upon purple with sandals of gold, of placing the diadem upon the brows of the fairest of women.

These thoughts made his blood boil in his veins, and, as though to pursue the flight of his dreams, he smote his sinewy heel upon the foam-whitened flanks of his Numidian horse.

The weather, at first calm, had changed and waxed tempestuous like the warrior's soul; and Boreas, his locks bristling with Thracian frosts, his cheeks puffed out, his arms folded upon his breast, smote the rain-freighted clouds with the mighty beatings of his wings.

A bevy of young girls who had been gathering flowers in the meadow, fearing the coming storm, were returning to the city in all haste, each carrying her perfumed harvest in the lap of her tunic. Seeing a stranger on horseback approaching in the distance, they had hidden their faces in their mantles, after the custom of the barbarians; but at the very moment that Gyges was passing by the one whose proud carriage and richer habiliments seemed to designate her the mistress of the little band, an unusually violent gust of wind carried away the veil of the fair unknown, and, whirling it through the air like a feather, chased it to such a distance that it could not be recovered. It was Nyssia, daughter of Megabazus, who found herself thus with face unveiled in the presence of Gyges, a humble captain of King Candaules's guard. Was it only the breath of Boreas which had brought about this accident, or had Eros, who delights to vex the hearts of men, amused himself by severing the string which had fastened the protecting tissue? However that may have been, Gyges was stricken motionless at the sight of that Medusa of beauty, and not till long after the folds of Nyssia's robe had disappeared beyond the gates of the city could he think of proceeding on his way. Although there was nothing to justify such a conjecture, he cherished the belief that he had seen the satrap's daughter; and that meeting, which affected him almost like an apparition, accorded so fully with the thoughts that were occupying him at the moment of its occurrence, that he could not help perceiving therein something fateful and ordained of the gods. In truth it was upon that brow that he would have wished to place the diadem. What other could be more worthy of it? But what probability was there that Gyges would ever have a throne to share? He had not sought to follow up this adventure, and assure himself that it was indeed the daughter of Megabazus whose mysterious face had been revealed to him by Chance, the great filcher. Nyssia had fled so swiftly that it would have been impossible for him then to overtake her; and, moreover, he had been dazzled, fascinated, thunder-stricken, as it were, rather than charmed by that superhuman apparition, by that monster of beauty!

Nevertheless that image, although seen only in the glimpse of a moment, had engraved itself upon his heart in lines deep as those which the sculptors trace on ivory with tools reddened in the fire. He had endeavoured, although vainly, to efface it, for the love which he felt for Nyssia inspired him with a secret terror. Perfection in such a degree is ever awe-inspiring, and women so like unto goddesses could only work evil to feeble mortals; they are formed for divine adulteries, and even the most courageous men never risk themselves in such amours without trembling. Therefore no hope had blossomed in the soul of Gyges, overwhelmed and discouraged in advance by the sentiment of the impossible. Ere opening his lips to Nyssia he would have wished to despoil the heaven of its robe of stars, to take from Phoebus his crown of rays, forgetting that women only give themselves to those unworthy of them, and that to win their love one must act as though he desired to earn their hate.

From that day the roses of joy no longer bloomed upon his cheeks. By day he was sad and mournful, and seemed to wander abroad in solitary dreaming, like a mortal who has beheld a divinity. At night he was haunted by dreams in which he beheld Nyssia seated by his side upon cushions of purple between the golden griffins of the royal throne.

Therefore Gyges, the only one who could speak of his own knowledge concerning Nyssia, having never spoken of her, the Sardians were left to their own conjectures in her regard; and their conjectures, it must be confessed, were fantastic and altogether fabulous. The beauty of Nyssia, thanks to the veils which shrouded her, became a sort of myth, a canvas, a poem to which each one added ornamentation as the fancy took him.

'If report be not false,' lisped a young debauchee from Athens, who stood with one hand upon the shoulder of an Asiatic boy, 'neither Plangon, nor Archianassa, nor Thais can be compared with this marvellous barbarian; yet I can scarce believe that she equals Theano of Colophon, from whom I once bought a single night at the price of as much gold as she could bear away, after having plunged both her white arms up to the shoulder in my cedar-wood coffer.'

'Beside her,' added a Eupatrid, who pretended to be better informed than any other person upon all manner of subjects, 'beside her the daughter of Coelus and the Sea would seem but a mere Ethiopian servant.'

'Your words are blasphemy, and although Aphrodite be a kind and indulgent goddess, beware of drawing down her anger upon you.'

'By Hercules!—and that ought to be an oath of some weight in a city ruled by one of his descendants—I cannot retract a word of it.'

'You have seen her, then?'

'No; but I have a slave in my service who once belonged to Nyssia, and who has told me a hundred stories about her.'

'Is it true,' demanded in infantile tones an equivocal-looking woman whose pale-rose tunic, painted cheeks, and locks shining with essences betrayed wretched pretensions to a youth long passed away—' is it true that Nyssia has two pupils in each eye? It seems to me that must be very ugly, and I cannot understand how Candaules could fall in love with such a monstrosity, while there is no lack, at Sardes and in Lydia, of women whose eyes are irreproachable.'

And uttering these words with all sorts of affected airs and simperings, Lamia took a little significant peep in a small mirror of cast metal which she drew from her bosom, and which enabled her to lead back to duty certain wandering curls disarranged by the impertinence of the wind.

'As to the double pupil, that seems to me nothing more than an old nurse's tale,' observed the well-informed patrician; 'but it is a fact that Nyssia's eyes are so piercing that she can see through walls. Lynxes are myopic compared with her.'

'How can a sensible man coolly argue about such an absurdity?' interrupted a citizen, whose bald skull, and the flood of snowy beard into which he plunged his fingers while speaking, lent him an air of preponderance and philosophical sagacity. 'The truth is that the daughter of Megabazus cannot naturally see through a wall any better than you or I, but the Egyptian priest Thoutmosis, who knows so many wondrous secrets, has given her the mysterious stone which is found in the heads of dragons, and whose property, as every one knows, renders all shadows and the most opaque bodies transparent to the eyes of those who possess it. Nyssia always carries this stone in her girdle, or else set into her bracelet, and in that may be found the secret of her clairvoyance.'

The citizen's explanation seemed the most natural one to those of the group whose conversation we are endeavouring to reproduce, and the opinions of Lamia and the patrician were abandoned as improbable.

'At all events,' returned the lover of Theano, 'we are going to have an opportunity of judging for ourselves, for it seems to me that I hear the clarions sounding in the distance, and though Nyssia is still invisible, I can see the herald yonder approaching with palm branches in his hands, to announce the arrival of the nuptial *cortége*, and make the crowd fall back.'

At this news, which spread rapidly through the crowd, the strong men elbowed their way toward the front ranks; the agile boys, embracing the shafts of the columns, sought to climb up to the capitals and there seat themselves; others, not without having skinned their knees against the bark, succeeded in perching themselves comfortably enough in the Y of some tree-branch. The women lifted their little children upon their shoulders, warning them to hold tightly to their necks. Those who had the good fortune to dwell on the street along which Candaules and Nyssia were about to pass, leaned over from the summit of their roofs, or, rising on their elbows, abandoned for a time the cushions upon which they had been reclining.

A murmur of satisfaction and gratified expectation ran through the crowd, which had already been waiting many long hours, for the arrows of the midday sun were commencing to sting.

The heavy-armed warriors, with cuirasses of bull's-hide covered with overlapping plates of metal, helmets adorned with plumes of horse-hair dyed red, *knemides* or greaves faced with tin, baldrics studded with nails, emblazoned bucklers, and swords of brass, rode behind a line of trumpeters who blew with might and main upon their long tubes, which gleamed under the sunlight. The horses of these warriors were all white as the feet of Thetis, and might have served, by reason of their noble paces and purity of breeds, as models for those which Phidias at a later day sculptured upon the metopes of the Parthenon.

At the head of this troop rode Gyges, the well-named, for his name in the Lydian tongue signifies beautiful. His features, of the most exquisite regularity, seemed chiselled in marble, owing to his intense pallor, for he had just discovered in Nyssia, although she was veiled with the veil of a young bride, the same woman whose face had been betrayed to his gaze by the treachery of Boreas under the walls of Bactria.

'Handsome Gyges looks very sad,' said the young maidens. 'What proud beauty could have secured his love, or what forsaken one has caused some Thessalian witch to cast a spell on him? Has that cabalistic ring (which he is said to have found hidden within the flanks of a brazen horse in the midst of some forest) lost its virtue, and suddenly ceasing to render its owner invisible, betrayed him to the astonished eyes of some innocent husband, who had deemed himself alone in his conjugal chamber?'

'Perhaps he has been wasting his talents and his drachmas at the game of Palamedes, or else it may be that he is disappointed at not having won the prize at the Olympian games. He had great faith in his horse Hyperion.'

No one of these conjectures was true. A fact is never guessed.

After the battalion commanded by Gyges, there came young boys crowned with myrtle-wreaths, and singing epithalamic hymns after the Lydian manner, accompanying themselves upon lyres of ivory, which they played with bows. All were clad in rose-coloured tunics ornamented with a silver Greek border, and their long hair flowed down over their shoulders in thick curls.

They preceded the gift-bearers, strong slaves whose half-nude bodies exposed to view such interlacements of muscle as the stoutest athletes might have envied.

Upon brancards, supported by two or four men or more, according to the weight of the objects borne, were placed enormous brazen cratera, chiselled by the most famous artists; vases of gold and silver whose sides were adorned with bas-reliefs and whose hands were elegantly worked into chimeras, foliage, and nude women; magnificent ewers to be used in washing the feet of illustrious guests; flagons encrusted with precious stones and containing the rarest perfumes; myrrh from Arabia, cinnamon from the Indies, spikenard from Persia, essence of roses from Smyrna; kamklins or perfuming pans, with perforated covers; cedar-wood or ivory coffers of marvellous workmanship, which opened with a secret spring that none save the inventor could find, and which contained bracelets wrought from the gold of Ophir, necklaces of the most lustrous pearls, mantle-brooches constellated with rubies and carbuncles; toilet-boxes, containing blond sponges, curling-irons, sea-wolves' teeth to polish the nails, the green rouge of Egypt, which turns to a most beautiful pink on touching the skin, powders to darken the eyelashes and eyebrows, and all the refinements that feminine coquetry could invent. Other litters were freighted with purple robes of the finest linen and of all possible shades from the incarnadine hue of the rose to the deep crimson of the blood of the grape; *calasires* of the linen of Canopus, which is thrown all white into the vat of the dyer, and comes forth again, owing to the various astringents in which it had been steeped, diapered with the most brilliant colours; tunics brought from the fabulous land of Seres, made from the spun slime of a worm which feeds upon leaves, and so fine that they might be drawn through a finger-ring.

Ethiopians, whose bodies shone like jet, and whose temples were tightly bound with cords, lest they should burst the veins of their foreheads in the effort to uphold their burden, carried in great pomp a statue of Hercules, the ancestor of Candaules, of colossal size, wrought of ivory and gold, with the club, the skin of the Nemean lion, the three apples from the garden of the Hesperides, and all the traditional attributes of the hero.

Statues of Venus Urania, and of Venus Genitrix, sculptured by the best pupils of the Sicyon School. That marble of Paros whose gleaming transparency seemed expressly created for the representation of the ever-youthful flesh of the immortals, were borne after the statue of Hercules, which admirably relieved the harmony and elegance of their proportions by contrast with its massive outlines and rugged forms.

A painting by Bularchus, which Candaules had purchased for its weight in gold, executed upon the wood of the female larch-tree, and representing the defeat of the Magnesians, evoked universal admiration by the beauty of its design, the truthfulness of the attitude of its figures, and the harmony of its colouring, although the artist had only employed in its production the four primitive colours: Attic ochre, white, Pontic *sinopis* and *atramentum*. The young king loved painting and sculpture even more, perhaps, than well became a monarch, and he had not unfrequently bought a picture at a price equal to the annual revenue of a whole city.

Camels and dromedaries, splendidly caparisoned, with musicians seated on their necks performing upon drums and cymbals, carried the gilded stakes, the cords, and the material of the tent designed for the use of the queen during voyages and hunting parties.

These spectacles of magnificence would upon any other occasion have ravished the people of Sardes with delight, but their curiosity had been enlisted in another direction, and it was not without a certain feeling of impatience that they watched this portion of the procession file by. The young maidens and the handsome boys, bearing flaming torches, and strewing handfuls of crocus flowers along the way, hardly attracted any attention. The idea of beholding Nyssia had preoccupied all minds.

At last Candaules appeared, riding in a chariot drawn by four horses, as beautiful and spirited as those of the sun, all rolling their golden bits in foam, shaking their purple-decked manes, and restrained with great difficulty by the driver, who stood erect at the side of Candaules, and was leaning back to gain more power on the reins.

Candaules was a young man full of vigour, and well worthy of his Herculean origin. His head was joined to his shoulders by a neck massive as a bull's, and almost without a curve; his hair, black and lustrous, twisted itself into rebellious little curls, here and there concealing the circlet of his diadem; his ears, small and upright, were of a ruddy hue; his forehead was broad and full, though a little low, like all antique foreheads; his eyes full of gentle melancholy, his oval cheeks, his chin with its gentle and regular curves, his mouth with its slightly parted lips—all bespoke the nature of the poet rather than that of the warrior. In fact, although he was brave, skilled in all bodily exercises, could subdue a wild horse as well as any of the Lapithæ, or swim across the current of rivers when they descended, swollen with melted snow, from the mountains, although he might have bent the bow of Odysseus or borne the shield of Achilles, he seemed little occupied with dreams of conquest; and war usually so fascinating to young kings, had little attraction for him. He contented himself with repelling the attacks of his ambitious neighbours, and sought not to extend his own dominions. He preferred building palaces, after plans suggested by himself to the architects, who always found the king's hints of no small value, or to form collections of statues and paintings by artists of the elder and later schools. He had the works of Telephanes of Sicyon, Cleanthes, Ardices of Corinth, Hygiemon, Deinias, Charmides, Eumarus, and Cimon, some being simple drawings, and others paintings in various colours or monochromes. It was even said that Candaules had not disdained to wield with his own royal hands—a thing hardly becoming a prince—the chisel of the sculptor and the sponge of the encaustic painter.

But why should we dwell upon Candaules? The reader undoubtedly feels like the people of Sardes: and it is of Nyssia that he desires to hear.

The daughter of Megabazus was mounted upon an elephant, with wrinkled skin and immense ears which seemed like flags, who advanced with a heavy but rapid gait, like a vessel in the midst of the waves. His tusks and his trunk were encircled with silver rings, and around the pillars of his limbs were entwined necklaces of enormous pearls. Upon his back, which was covered with a magnificent Persian carpet of striped pattern, stood a sort of estrade overlaid with gold finely chased, and constellated with onyx stones, carnelians, chrysolites, lapis-lazuli, and girasols; upon this estrade sat the young queen, so covered with precious stones as to dazzle the eyes of the beholders. A mitre, shaped like a helmet, on which pearls formed flower designs and letters after the Oriental manner, was placed upon her head; her ears, both the lobes and rims of which had been pierced, were adorned with ornaments in the form of little cups, crescents, and balls; necklaces of gold and silver beads, which had been hollowed out and carved, thrice encircled her neck and descended with a metallic tinkling upon her bosom; emerald serpents with topaz or ruby eyes coiled themselves in many folds about her arms, and clasped themselves by biting their own tails. These bracelets were connected by chains of precious stones, and so great was their weight that two attendants were required to kneel beside Nyssia and support her elbows. She was clad in a robe embroidered by Syrian workmen with shining designs of golden foliage and diamond fruits, and over this she wore the short tunic of Persepolis, which hardly descended to the knee, and of which the sleeves were slit and fastened by sapphire clasps. Her waist was encircled from hip to loins by a girdle wrought of narrow material, variegated with stripes and flowered designs, which formed themselves into symmetrical patterns as they were brought together by a certain arrangement of the folds which Indian girls alone know how to make. Her trousers of byssus, which the Phoenicians called *syndon* were confined at the ankles by anklets adorned with gold and silver bells, and completed this toilet so fantastically rich and wholly opposed to Greek taste. But, alas! a saffron-coloured *flammeum* pitilessly masked the face of Nyssia, who seemed embarrassed, veiled though she was, at finding so many eyes fixed upon her, and frequently signed to a slave behind her to lower the parasol of ostrich plumes, and thus conceal her yet more from the curious gaze of the crowd.

Candaules had vainly begged of her to lay aside her veil, even for that solemn occasion. The young barbarian had refused to pay the welcome of her beauty to his people. Great was the disappointment. Lamia declared that Nyssia dared not uncover her face for fear of showing her double pupil. The young libertine remained convinced that Theano of Colophon was more beautiful than the queen of Sardes; and Gyges sighed when he beheld Nyssia, after having made her elephant kneel down, descend upon the inclined heads of Damascus slaves as upon a living ladder, to the threshold of the royal dwelling, where the elegance of Greek architecture was blended with the fantasies and enormities of Asiatic taste.

CHAPTER II

In our character of poet we have the right to lift the saffron-coloured *flammeum* which concealed the young bride, being more fortunate in this wise than the Sardians, who after a whole day's waiting were obliged to return to their houses, and were left, as before, to their own conjectures.

Nyssia was really far superior to her reputation, great as it was. It seemed as though Nature in creating her had resolved to exhaust her utmost powers, and thus make atonement for all former experimental attempts and fruitless essays. One would have said that, moved by jealousy of the future marvels of the Greek sculptors, she also had resolved to model a statue herself, and to prove that she was still sovereign mistress in the plastic art.

The grain of snow, the micaceous brilliancy of Parian marble, the sparkling pulp of balsamine flowers, would render but a feeble idea of the ideal substance whereof Nyssia had been formed. That flesh, so fine, so delicate, permitted daylight to penetrate it, and modelled itself in transparent contours, in lines as sweetly harmonious as music itself. According to different surroundings, it took the colour of the sunlight or of purple, like the aromal body of a divinity, and seemed to radiate light and life. The world of perfections inclosed within the nobly lengthened oval of her chaste face could have been rendered by no earthly art—neither by the chisel of the sculptor, nor the brush of the painter, nor the style of any poet—though it were Praxiteles, Apelles, or Mimnernus; and on her smooth brow, bathed by waves of hair amber-bright as molten electrum and sprinkled with gold filings, according to the Babylonian custom, sat as upon a jasper throne the unalterable serenity of perfect loveliness.

As for her eyes, though they did not justify what popular credulity said of them, they were at least wonderfully strange eyes;

brown eyebrows, with extremities ending in points elegant as those of the arrows of Eros, and which were joined to each other by a streak of henna after the Asiatic fashion, and long fringes of silkily-shadowed eyelashes contrasted strikingly with the twin sapphire stars rolling in the heaven of dark silver which formed those eyes. The irises of those eyes, whose pupils were blacker than atrament, varied singularly in shades of shifting colour. From sapphire they changed to turquoise, from turquoise to beryl, from beryl to yellow amber, and sometimes, like a limpid lake whose bottom is strewn with jewels, they offered, through their incalculable depths, glimpses of golden and diamond sands upon which green fibrils vibrated and twisted themselves into emerald serpents. In those orbs of phosphoric lightning the rays of suns extinguished, the splendours of vanished worlds, the glories of Olympus eclipsed—all seemed to have concentrated their reflections. When contemplating them one thought of eternity, and felt himself seized with a mighty giddiness, as though he were leaning over the verge of the Infinite.

The expression of those extraordinary eyes was not less variable than their tint. At times their lids opened like the portals of celestial dwellings; they invited you into elysiums of light, of azure, of ineffable felicity; they promised you the realisation, tenfold, a hundredfold, of all your dreams of happiness, as though they had divined your soul's most secret thoughts; again, impenetrable as sevenfold plated shields of the hardest metals, they flung back your gaze like blunted and broken arrows. With a simple inflexion of the brow, a mere flash of the pupil, more terrible than the thunder of Zeus, they precipitated you from the heights of your most ambitious escalades into depths of nothingness so profound that it was impossible to rise again. Typhon himself, who writhes under Ætna, could not have lifted the mountains of disdain with which they overwhelmed you. One felt that though he should live for a thousand Olympiads endowed with the beauty of the fair son of Latona, the genius of Orpheus, the unbounded might of Assyrian kings, the treasures of the Cabeirei, the Telchines, and the Dactyli, gods of subterranean wealth, he could never change their expression to mildness.

At other times their languishment was so liquidly persuasive, their brilliancy and irradiation so penetrating, that the icy coldness of Nestor and Priam would have melted under their gaze, like the wax of the wings of Icarus when he approached the flaming zones. For one such glance a man would have gladly steeped his hands in the blood of his host, scattered the ashes of his father to the four winds, overthrown the holy images of the gods, and stolen the fire of heaven itself, like the sublime thief, Prometheus.

Nevertheless, their most ordinary expression, it must be confessed, was of a chastity to make one desperate—a sublime coldness—an ignorance of all possibilities of human passion, such as would have made the moon-bright eyes of Phoebe or the sea-green eyes of Athena appear by comparison more liquidly tempting than those of a young girl of Babylon sacrificing to the goddess Mylitta within the cord-circled enclosure of Succoth-Benohl. Their invincible virginity seemed to bid love defiance.

The cheeks of Nyssia, which no human gaze had ever profaned, save that of Gyges on the day when the veil was blown away, possessed a youthful bloom, a tender pallor, a delicacy of grain, and a downiness whereof the faces of our women, perpetually exposed to sunlight and air, cannot convey the most distant idea. Modesty created fleeting rosy clouds upon them like those which a drop of crimson essence would form in a cup of milk, and when uncoloured by any emotion they took a silvery sheen, a warm light, like an alabaster vessel illumined by a lamp within. That lamp was her charming soul, which exposed to view the transparency of her flesh.

A bee would have been deceived by her mouth, whose form was so perfect, whose corners were so purely dimpled, whose crimson was so rich and warm that the gods would have descended from their Olympian dwellings in order to touch it with lips humid with immortality, but that the jealousy of the goddesses restrained their impetuosity. Happy the wind which passed through that purple and pearl, which dilated those pretty nostrils, so finely cut and shaded with rosy tints like the mother-of-pearl of the shells thrown by the sea on the shore of Cyprus at the feet of Venus Anadyomene! But are there not a multitude of favours thus granted to things which cannot understand them? What lover would not wish to be the tunic of his well-beloved or the water of her bath?

Such was Nyssia, if we dare make use of the expression after so vague a description of her face. If our foggy Northern idioms had the warm liberty, the burning enthusiasm of the Sir Hasirim, we might, perhaps, by comparisons—awakening in the mind of the reader memories of flowers and perfumes, of music and sunlight, evoking, by the magic of words, all the graceful and charming images that the universe can contain—have been able to give some idea of Nyssia's features; but it is permitted to Solomon alone to compare the nose of a beautiful woman to the tower of Lebanon which looketh toward Damascus. And yet what is there in the world of more importance than the nose of a beautiful woman? Had Helen, the white Tyndarid, been flat-nosed, would the Trojan War have taken place? And if the profile of Semiramis had not been perfectly regular, would she have bewitched the old monarch of Nineveh and encircled her brow with the mitre of pearls, the symbol of supreme power?

Although Candaules had brought to his palace the most beautiful slaves from the people of the Sorse, of Askalon, of Sogdiana, of the Sacse, of Rhapta, the most celebrated courtesans from Ephesus, from Pergamus, from Smyrna, and from Cyprus, he was completely fascinated by the charms of Nyssia. Up to that time he had not even suspected the existence of such perfection.

Privileged as a husband to enjoy fully the contemplation of this beauty, he found himself dazzled, giddy, like one who leans over the edge of an abyss, or fixes his eyes upon the sun; he felt himself seized, as it were, with the dilirium of possession, like a priest drunk with the god who fills and moves him. All other thoughts disappeared from his soul, and the universe seemed to him only as a vague mist in the midst of which beamed the shining phantom of Nyssia. His happiness transformed itself into ecstasy, and his love into madness. At times his very felicity terrified him. To be only a wretched king, only a remote descendant of a hero who had become a god by mighty labours, only a common man formed of flesh and bone, and without having in aught rendered himself worthy of it—without having even, like his ancestor, strangled some hydra, or torn some lion asunder—to enjoy a happiness whereof Zeus of the ambrosial hair would scarce be worthy, though lord of all Olympus! He felt, as it were, a shame to thus hoard up for himself alone so rich a treasure, to steal this marvel from the world, to be the dragon with scales and claws who guarded the living type of the ideal of lovers, sculptors, and poets. All they had ever dreamed of in their hope, their melancholy, and their despair, he possessed—

he, Candaules, poor tyrant of Sardes, who had only a few wretched coffers filled with pearls, a few cisterns filled with gold pieces, and thirty or forty thousand slaves, purchased or taken in war.

Candaules's felicity was too great for him, and the strength which he would doubtless have found at his command in time of misfortune was wanting to him in time of happiness. His joy overflowed from his soul like water from a vase placed upon the fire, and in the exasperation of his enthusiasm for Nyssia he had reached the point of desiring that she were less timid and less modest, for it cost him no little effort to retain in his own breast the secret of such wondrous beauty.

'Ah,' he would murmur to himself during the deep reveries which absorbed him at all hours that he did not spend at the queen's side, 'how strange a lot is mine! I am wretched because of that which would make any other husband happy. Nyssia will not leave the shadow of the gynaeceum, and refuses, with barbarian modesty, to lift her veil in the presence of any other than myself. Yet with what an intoxication of pride would my love behold her, radiantly sublime, gaze down upon my kneeling people from the summit of the royal steps, and, like the rising dawn, extinguish all those pale stars who during the night thought themselves suns! Proud Lydian women, who believe yourselves beautiful, but for Nyssia's reserve you would appear, even to your lovers, as ugly as the oblique-eyed and thick-lipped slaves of Nahasi and Kush. Were she but once to pass along the streets of Sardes with face unveiled, you might in vain pull your adorers by the lappet of their tunic, for none of them would turn his head, or, if he did, it would be to demand your name, so utterly would he have forgotten you! They would rush to precipitate themselves beneath the silver wheels of her chariot, that they might have even the pleasure of being crushed by her, like those devotees of the Indus who pave the pathway of their idol with their bodies.

'And you, O goddesses, whom Paris-Alexander judged, had Nyssia appeared among you, not one of you would have borne away the golden apple, not even Aphrodite, despite her cestus and her promise to the shepherd-arbiter that she would make him beloved by the most beautiful woman in the world! . . .

'Alas! to think that such beauty is not immortal, and that years will alter those divine outlines, that admirable hymn of forms, that poem whose strophes are contours, and which no one in the world has ever read or may ever read save myself; to be the sole depositary of so splendid a treasure! If I knew even by imitating the play of light and shadow with the aid of lines and colours, how to fix upon wood a reflection of that celestial face; if marble were not rebellious to my chisel, how well would I fashion in the purest vein of Paros or Pentelicus an image of that charming body, which would make the proud effigies of the goddesses fall from their altars! And long after, when deep below the slime of deluges, and beneath the dust of ruined cities, the men of future ages should find a fragment of that petrified shadow of Nyssia, they would cry: "Behold, how the women of this vanished world were formed!" And they would erect a temple wherein to enshrine the divine fragment. But I have naught save a senseless admiration and a love that is madness! Sole adorer of an unknown divinity, I possess no power to spread her worship through the world.'

Thus in Candaules had the enthusiasm of the artist extinguished the jealousy of the lover. Admiration was mightier than love. If in place of Nyssia, daughter of the Satrap Megabazus, all imbued with Oriental ideas, he had espoused some Greek girl from Athens or Corinth, he would certainly have invited to his court the most skilful painters and sculptors, and have given them the queen for their model, as did afterward Alexander his favourite Campaspe, who posed naked before Apelles. Such a whim would have encountered no opposition from a woman of the land where even the most chaste made a boast of having contributed—some for the back, some for the bosom—to the perfection of a famous statue. But hardly would the bashful Nyssia consent to unveil herself in the discreet shadow of the thalamus, and the earnest prayers of the king really shocked her rather than gave her pleasure. The sentiment of duty and obedience alone induced her to yield at times to what she styled the whims of Candaules.

Sometimes he besought her to allow the flood of her hair to flow over her shoulders in a river of gold richer than the Pactolus, to encircle her brow with a crown of ivy and linden leaves like a bacchante of Mount Maenalus, to lie, hardly veiled by a cloud of tissue finer than woven wind, upon a tiger-skin with silver claws and ruby eyes, or to stand erect in a great shell of mother-of-pearl, with a dew of pearls falling from her tresses in lieu of drops of sea-water.

When he had placed himself in the best position for observation, he became absorbed in silent contemplation. His hand, tracing vague contours in the air, seemed to be sketching the outlines for some picture, and he would have remained thus for whole hours if Nyssia, soon becoming weary of her rôle of model, had not reminded him in chill and disdainful tones that such amusements were unworthy of royal majesty and contrary to the holy laws of matrimony. 'It is thus,' she would exclaim, as she withdrew, draped to her very eyes, into the most mysterious recesses of her apartment, 'that one treats a mistress, not a virtuous woman of noble blood!'

These wise remonstrances did not cure Candaules, whose passion augmented in inverse ratio to the coldness shown him by the queen. And it had at last brought him to that point that he could no longer keep the secrets of the nuptial couch. A confidant became as necessary to him as to the prince of a modern tragedy. He did not proceed, you may feel assured, to fix his choice upon some crabbed philosopher of frowning mien, with a flood of gray-and-white beard rolling down over a mantle in proud tatters; nor a warrior who could talk of nothing save ballista, catapults, and scythed chariots; nor a sententious Eupatrid full of councils and politic maxims; but Gyges, whose reputation for gallantry caused him to be regarded as a connoisseur in regard to women.

One evening he laid his hand upon his shoulder in a more than ordinarily familiar and cordial manner, and after giving him a look of peculiar significance, he suddenly strode away from the group of courtiers, saying in a loud voice:

'Gyges, come and give me your opinion in regard to my effigy, which the Sicyon sculptors have just finished chiselling on the genealogical bas-relief where the deeds of my ancestors are celebrated.'

'O king, your knowledge is greater than that of your humble subject, and I know not how to express my gratitude for the honour you do me in deigning to consult me,' replied Gyges, with a sign of assent.

Candaules and his favourite traversed several halls ornamented in the Hellenic style, where the Corinthian acanthus and the Ionic volute bloomed or curled in the capitals of the columns, where the friezes were peopled with little figures in polychromatic plastique representing processions and sacrifices, and they finally arrived at a remote portion of the ancient palace whose walls were built with stones of irregular form, put together without cement in the cyclopean manner. This ancient architecture was colossally proportioned and weirdly grim. The immeasurable genius of the elder civilisations of the Orient was there legibly written, and recalled the granite and brick debauches of Egypt and Assyria. Something of the spirit of the ancient architects of the tower of Lylax survived in those thick-set pillars with their deep-fluted trunks, whose capitals were formed by four heads of bulls, placed forehead to forehead, and bound together by knots of serpents that seemed striving to devour them, an obscure cosmogonie symbol whereof the meaning was no longer intelligible, and had descended into the tomb with the hierophants of preceding ages. The gates were neither of a square nor rounded form. They described a sort of ogive much resembling the mitre of the Magi, and by their fantastic character gave still more intensity to the character of the building.

This portion of the palace formed a sort of court surrounded by a portico whose architecture was ornamented with the genealogical bas-relief to which Can-daules had alluded.

In the midst thereof sat Heracles upon a throne, with the upper part of his body uncovered, and his feet resting upon a stool, according to the rite for the representation of divine personages. His colossal proportions would otherwise have left no doubt as to his apotheosis, and the archaic rudeness and hugeness of the work, wrought by the chisel of some primitive artist, imparted to his figure an air of barbaric majesty, a savage grandeur more appropriate, perhaps, to the character of this monster-slaying hero than would have been the work of a sculptor consummate in his art.

On the right of the throne were Alcseus, son of the hero and of Omphale; Ninus, Belus, Argon, the earlier kings of the dynasty of the Heracleidae, then all the line of intermediate kings, terminating with Ardys, Alyattes, Meles or Myrsus, father of Candaules, and finally Candaules himself.

All these personages, with their hair braided into little strings, their beards spirally twisted, their oblique eyes, angular attitudes, cramped and stiff gestures, seemed to own a sort of factitious life, due to the rays of the setting sun, and the ruddy hue which time lends to marble in warm climates. The inscriptions in antique characters, graven beside them after the manner of legends, enhanced still more the mysterious weirdness of the long procession of figures in strange barbarian garb.

By a singular chance, which Gyges could not help observing, the statue of Candaules occupied the last available place at the right hand of Heracles; the dynastic cycle was closed, and in order to find a place for the descendants of Candaules it would be absolutely necessary to build a new portico and commence the formation of a new bas-relief.

Candaules, whose arm still rested on the shoulder of Gyges, walked slowly round the portico in silence. He seemed to hesitate to enter into the subject, and had altogether forgotten the pretext under which he had led the captain of his guards into that solitary place.

'What would you do, Gyges,' said Candaules, at last breaking the silence which had been growing painful to both, 'if you were a diver, and should bring up from the green bosom of the ocean a pearl of incomparable purity and lustre, and of worth so vast as to exhaust the richest treasures of the earth?'

'I would inclose it,' answered Gyges, a little surprised at this brusque question, 'in a cedar box overlaid with plates of brass, and I would bury it under a detached rock in some desert place; and from time to time, when I should feel assured that none could see me, I would go thither to contemplate my precious jewel and admire the colours of the sky mingling with its nacreous tints.'

'And I,' replied Candaules, his eye illuminated with enthusiasm, 'if I possessed so rich a gem, I would enshrine it in my diadem, that I might exhibit it freely to the eyes of all men, in the pure light of the sun, that I might adorn myself with its splendour and smile with pride when I should hear it said: "Never did king of Assyria or Babylon, never did Greek or Trinacrian tyrant possess so lustrous a pearl as Candaules, son of Myrsus and descendant of Heracles, King of Sardes and of Lydia! Compared with Candaules, Midas, who changed all things to gold, were only a mendicant as poor as Irus."'

Gyges listened with astonishment to this discourse of Candaules, and sought to penetrate the hidden sense of these lyric divagations. The king appeared to be in a state of extraordinary excitement: his eyes sparkled with enthusiasm; a feverish rosiness tinted his cheeks; his dilated nostrils inhaled the air with unusual effort.

'Well, Gyges,' continued Candaules, without appearing to notice the uneasiness of his favourite, 'I am that diver. Amid this dark ocean of humanity, wherein confusedly move so many defective or misshapen beings, so many forms incomplete or degraded, so many types of bestial ugliness, wretched outlines of nature's experimental essays, I have found beauty, pure, radiant, without spot, without flaw, the ideal made real, the dream accomplished, a form which no painter or sculptor has ever been able to translate upon canvas or into marble—I have found Nyssia!'

'Although the queen has the timid modesty of the women of the Orient, and that no man save her husband has ever beheld her features, Fame, hundred-tongued and hundred-eared, has celebrated her praise throughout the world,' answered Gyges, respectfully inclining his head as he spoke.

'Mere vague, insignificant rumours. They say of her, as of all women not actually ugly, that she is more beautiful than Aphrodite or Helen; but no person could form even the most remote idea of such perfection. In vain have I besought Nyssia to appear unveiled at some public festival, some solemn sacrifice, or to show herself for an instant leaning over the royal terrace, bestowing upon her people the immense favour of one look, the prodigality of one profile view, more generous than the goddesses who permit their worshippers to behold only pale simulacra of ivory or alabaster. She would never consent to that. Now there is one strange thing which I blush to acknowledge even to you, dear Gyges. Formerly I was jealous; I wished to conceal my amours from all eyes, no shadow was thick enough, no mystery sufficiently impenetrable. Now I can no longer recognise myself. I have the feelings neither of a lover nor a husband; my love has melted in adoration like thin wax in a fiery brazier. All petty feelings of jealousy or possession have vanished. No, the most finished work that heaven has ever given to earth, since the day that Prometheus held the flame under the right breast of the statue of clay, cannot thus be kept hidden in the chill shadow of the gynaeceum. Were I to die, then the secret of this beauty would for ever remain shrouded beneath the sombre draperies of widowhood! I feel myself culpable in its concealment, as though I had the sun in my house, and prevented it from illuminating the world. And when I think of those harmonious lines, those divine contours which I dare scarcely touch with a timid kiss, I feel my heart ready to burst; I wish that some friendly eye could share my happiness and, like a severe judge to whom a picture is shown, recognise after careful examination that it is irreproachable, and that the possessor has not been deceived by his enthusiasm. Yes, often do I feel myself tempted to tear off with rash hand those odious tissues, but Nyssia, in her fierce chastity, would never forgive me. And still I cannot alone endure such felicity. I must have a confidant for my ecstasies, an echo which will answer my cries of admiration, and it shall be none other than you.'

Having uttered these words, Candaules brusquely turned and disappeared through a secret passage. Gyges, left thus alone, could not avoid noticing the peculiar concourse of events which seemed to place him always in Nyssia's path. A chance had enabled him to behold her beauty, though walled up from all other eyes. Among many princes and satraps she had chosen to espouse Candaules, the very king he served; and through some strange caprice, which he could only regard as fateful, this king had just made him, Gyges, his confidant in regard to the mysterious creature whom none else had approached, and absolutely sought to complete the work of Boreas on the plain of Bactria! Was not the hand of the gods visible in all these circumstances? That spectre of beauty, whose veil seemed to be lifted slowly, a little at a time, as though to enkindle a flame within him, was it not leading him, without his having suspected it, toward the accomplishment of some mighty destiny? Such were the questions which Gyges asked himself, but being unable to penetrate the obscurity of the future, he resolved to await the course of events, and left the Court of Images, where the twilight darkness was commencing to pile itself up in all the angles, and to render the effigies of the ancestors of Candaules yet more and more weirdly menacing.

Was it a mere effort of light, or was it rather an illusion produced by that vague uneasiness with which the boldest hearts are filled by the approach of night amid ancient monuments? As he stepped across the threshold Gyges fancied that he heard deep groans issue from the stone lips of the bas-reliefs, and it seemed to him that Heracles was making enormous efforts to loosen his granite club.

CHAPTER III

On the following day Candaules again took Gyges aside and continued the conversation begun under the portico of the Heracleidæ. Having freed himself from the embarrassment of broaching the subject, he freely unbosomed himself to his confidant; and had Nyssia been able to overhear him she might perhaps have been willing to pardon his conjugal indiscretions for the sake of his passionate eulogies of her charms.

Gyges listened to all these bursts of praise with the slightly constrained air of one who is yet uncertain whether his interlocutor is not feigning an enthusiasm more ardent than he actually feels, in order to provoke a confidence naturally cautious to utter itself. Can-daules at last said to him in a tone of disappointment: 'I see, Gyges, that you do not believe me. You think I am boasting, or have allowed myself to be fascinated like some clumsy labourer by a robust country girl on whose cheeks Hygeia has crushed the gross hues of health. No, by all the gods! I have collected within my home, like a living bouquet, the fairest flowers of Asia and of Greece. I know all that the art of sculptors and painters has produced since the time of Daedalus, whose statues walked and spoke. Linus, Orpheus, Homer, have taught me harmony and rhythm. I do not look about me with Love's bandage blindfolding my eyes. I judge of all things coolly. The passions of youth never influence my admiration, and when I am as withered, decrepit, wrinkled, as Tithonus in his swaddling bands, my opinion will be still the same. But I forgive your incredulity and want of sympathy. In order to understand me fully, it is necessary that you should see Nyssia in the radiant brilliancy of her shining whiteness, free from jealous drapery, even as Nature with her own hands moulded her in a lost moment of inspiration which never can return. This evening

I will hide you in a corner of the bridal chamber . . . you shall see her!'

'Sire, what do you ask of me?' returned the young warrior with respectful firmness. 'How shall I, from the depths of my dust, from the abyss of my nothingness, dare to raise my eyes to this sun of perfections, at the risk of remaining blind for the rest of my life, or being able to see naught but a dazzling spectre in the midst of darkness? Have pity on your humble slave, and do not compel him to an action so contrary to the maxims of virtue. No man should look upon what does not belong to him. We know that the immortals always punish those who through imprudence or audacity surprise them in their divine nudity. Nyssia is the loveliest of all women; you are the happiest of lovers and husbands. Heracles, your ancestor, never found in the course of his many conquests aught to compare with your queen. If you, the prince of whom even the most skilful artists seek judgment and counsel—if you find her incomparable, of what consequence can the opinion of an obscure soldier like me be to you? Abandon, therefore, this fantasy, which I presume to say is unworthy of your royal majesty, and of which you would repent so soon as it had been satisfied.'

'Listen, Gyges,' returned Candaules; 'I perceive that you suspect me; you think that I seek to put you to some proof, but by the ashes of that funeral pyre whence my ancestor arose a god, I swear to you that I speak frankly and without any after-purpose.'

'O Candaules, I doubt not of your good faith; your passion is sincere, but perchance, after I should have obeyed you, you would conceive a deep aversion to me, and learn to hate me for not having more firmly resisted your will. You would seek to take back from these eyes, indiscreet through compulsion, the image which you allowed them to glance upon in a moment of delirium; and who knows but that you would condemn them to the eternal night of the tomb to punish them for remaining open at a moment when they ought to have been closed.'

'Fear nothing; I pledge my royal word that no evil shall befall you.'

'Pardon your slave if he still dares to offer some objection, even after such a promise. Have you reflected that what you propose to me is a violation of the sanctity of marriage, a species of visual adultery? A woman often lays aside her modesty with her garments;

and once violated by a look, without having actually ceased to be virtuous, she might deem that she had lost her flower of purity. You promise, indeed, to feel no resentment against me; but who can ensure me against the wrath of Nyssia, she who is so reserved and chaste, so apprehensive, fierce, and virginal in her modesty that she might be deemed still ignorant of the laws of Hymen? Should she ever learn of the sacrilege which I am about to render myself guilty of in deferring to my master's wishes, what punishment would she condemn me to suffer in expiation of such a crime? Who could place me beyond the reach of her avenging anger?'

'I did not know you were so wise and prudent,' said Candaules, with a slightly ironical smile; 'but such dangers are all imaginary, and I shall hide you in such a way that Nyssia will never know she has been seen by any one except her royal husband.'

Being unable to offer any further defence, Gyges made a sign of assent in token of complete submission to the king's will. He had made all the resistance in his power, and thenceforward his conscience could feel at ease in regard to whatever might happen; besides, by any further opposition to the will of Candaules, he would have feared to oppose destiny itself, which seemed striving to bring him still nearer to Nyssia for some grim ulterior purpose into which it was not given to him to see further.

Without actually being able to foresee any result, he beheld a thousand vague and shadowy images passing before his eyes. That subterranean love, so long crouched at the foot of his soul's stairway, had climbed a few steps higher, guided by some fitful glimmer of hope. The weight of the impossible no longer pressed so heavily upon his breast, now that he believed himself aided by the gods. In truth, who would have dreamed that the much-boasted charms of the daughter of Megabazus would ere long cease to own any mystery for Gyges?

'Come, Gyges,' said Candaules, taking him by the hand, 'let us make profit of the time. Nyssia is walking in the garden with her women; let us look at the place, and plan our stratagems for this evening.'

The king took his confidant by the hand and led him along the winding ways which conducted to the nuptial apartment. The doors of the sleeping-room were made of cedar planks so perfectly put together that it was impossible to discover the joints. By dint of rubbing them with wool steeped in oil, the slaves had rendered the wood as polished as marble. The brazen nails, with heads cut in facets, which studded them, had all the brilliancy of the purest gold. A complicated system of straps and metallic rings, whereof Candaules and his wife alone knew the combination, served to secure them, for in those heroic ages the locksmith's art was yet in its infancy.

Candaules unloosed the knots, made the rings slide back upon the thongs, raised with a handle which fitted into a mortise the bar that fastened the door from within, and bidding Gyges place himself against the wall, turned back one of the folding-doors upon him in such a way as to hide him completely; yet the door did not fit so perfectly to its frame of oaken beams, all carefully polished and put up according to line by a skilful workman, that the young warrior could not obtain a distinct view of the chamber interior through the interstices contrived to give room for the free play of the hinges.

Facing the entrance, the royal bed stood upon an estrade of several steps, covered with purple drapery. Columns of chased silver supported the entablature, all ornamented with foliage wrought in relief, amid which Loves were sporting with dolphins, and heavy curtains embroidered with gold surrounded it like the folds of a tent.

Upon the altar of the household gods were placed vases of precious metal, paterae enamelled with flowers, double-handled cups, and all things needful for libations.

Along the walls, which were faced with planks of cedar-wood, marvellously worked, at regular intervals stood tall statues of black basalt in the constrained attitudes of Egyptian art, each sustaining in its hand a bronze torch into which a splinter of resinous wood had been fitted.

An onyx lamp, suspended by a chain of silver, hung from that beam of the ceiling which is called the black beam, because more exposed than the others to the embrowning smoke. Every evening a slave carefully filled this lamp with odoriferous oil.

Near the head of the bed, on a little column, hung a trophy of arms, consisting of a visored helmet, a twofold buckler made of four bulls' hides and covered with plates of brass and tin, a two-edged sword, and several ashen javelins with brazen heads.

The tunics and mantles of Candaules were hung upon wooden pegs. They comprised garments both simple and double; that is, capable of going twice around the body. A mantle of thrice-dyed purple, ornamented with embroidery representing a hunting scene wherein Laconian hounds were pursuing and tearing deer, and a tunic whereof the material, fine and delicate as the skin which envelops an onion had all the sheen of woven sunbeams, were especially noticeable. Opposite to the trophy stood an armchair inlaid with silver and ivory upon which Nyssia hung her garments. Its seat was covered with a leopard skin more eye-spotted than the body of Argus, and its foot-support was richly adorned with openwork carving.

'I am generally the first to retire,' observed Candaules to Gyges, 'and I always leave this door open as it is now. Nyssia, who has invariably some tapestry flower to finish, or some order to give her women, usually delays a little in joining me; but at last she comes, and slowly takes off, one by one, as though the effort cost her dearly, and lays upon that ivory chair, all those draperies and tunics which by day envelop her like mummy bandages. From your hiding-place you will be able to follow all her graceful movements, admire her unrivalled charms, and judge for yourself whether Candaules be a young fool prone to vain boasting, or whether he does not really possess the richest pearl of beauty that ever adorned a diadem.'

'O King, I can well believe your words without such a proof as this,' replied Gyges, stepping forth from his hiding-place. 'When she has laid aside her garments,' continued Candaules, without heeding the exclamation of his confidant, 'she will come to lie down with me. You must take advantage of the moment to steal away, for in passing from the chair to the bed she turns her back to the door. Step lightly as though you were treading upon ears of ripe wheat; take heed that no grain of sand squeaks under your sandals; hold your breath, and retire as stealthily as possible. The vestibule is all in darkness, and the feeble rays of the only lamp which remains burning do not penetrate beyond the threshold of the chamber. It is, therefore, certain that Nyssia cannot possibly see you; and tomorrow there will be some one in the world who can comprehend my ecstasies, and will feel no longer astonished at my bursts of admiration. But see, the day is almost spent; the Sun will soon water his steeds in the Hesperian waves at the further end of the world, and beyond the Pillars erected by my ancestors. Return to your hiding-place, Gyges, and though the hours of waiting may seem long, I can swear by Eros of the Golden Arrows that you will not regret having waited.'

After this assurance Candaules left Gyges again hidden behind the door. The compulsory quiet which the king's young confidant found himself obliged to maintain left him ample leisure for thought. His situation was certainly a most extraordinary one. He had loved Nyssia as one loves a star. Convinced of the hopelessness of the undertaking, he had made no effort to approach her. And, nevertheless, by a succession of extraordinary events he was about to obtain a knowledge of treasures reserved for lovers and husbands only. Not a word, not a glance had been exchanged between himself and Nyssia, who probably ignored the very existence of the one being for whom her beauty would so soon cease to be a mystery. Unknown to her whose modesty would have naught to sacrifice for you, how strange a situation! To love a woman in secret and find oneself led by her husband to the threshold of the nuptial chamber, to have for guide to that treasure the very dragon who should defend all approach to it, was there not in all this ample food for astonishment and wonder at the combination of events wrought by destiny?

In the midst of these reflections, he suddenly heard the sound of footsteps on the pavement. It was only the slaves coming to replenish the oil in the lamp, throw fresh perfumes upon the coals of the kamklins, and arrange the purple and saffron-tinted sheepskins which formed the royal bed.

The hour approached, and Gyges felt his heart beat faster, and the pulsation of his arteries quicken. He even felt a strong impulse to steal away before the arrival of the queen, and, after averring subsequently to Candaules that he had remained, abandon himself confidently to the most extravagant eulogiums. He felt a strong repugnance (for, despite his somewhat free life, Gyges was not without delicacy) to take by stealth a favour for the free granting of which he would gladly have paid with his life. The husband's complicity rendered this theft more odious in a certain sense, and he would have preferred to owe to any other circumstance the happiness of beholding the marvel of Asia in her nocturnal toilet.

Perhaps, indeed, the approach of danger, let us acknowledge as veracious historians, had no little to do with his virtuous scruples. Undoubtedly Gyges did not lack courage. Mounted upon his war-chariot, with quiver rattling upon his shoulder, and bow in hand, he would have defied the most valiant warriors; in the chase he would have attacked without fear the Calydon boar or the Nemean lion; but—explain the enigma as you will—he trembled at the idea of looking at a beautiful woman through a chink in a door. No one possesses every kind of courage. He felt likewise that he could not behold Nyssia with impunity. It would be a decisive epoch in his life. Through having obtained but a momentary glimpse of her he had lost all peace of mind; what, then, would be the result of that which was about to take place? Could life itself continue for him when to that divine head which fired his dreams should be added a charming body formed for the kisses of the immortals? What would become of him should he find himself unable thereafter to contain his passion in darkness and silence as he had done till that time? Would he exhibit to the court of Lydia the ridiculous spectacle of an insane love, or would he strive by some extravagant action to bring down upon himself the disdainful pity of the queen? Such a result was strongly probable, since the reason of Candaules himself, the legitimate possessor of Nyssia, had been unable to resist the vertigo caused by that superhuman beauty—he, the thoughtless young king who till then had laughed at love, and preferred pictures and statues before all things. These arguments were very rational but wholly useless, for at the same moment Candaules entered the chamber, and exclaimed in a low but distinct voice as he passed the door:

'Patience, my poor Gyges, Nyssia will soon come.' When he saw that he could no longer retreat, Gyges, who was but a young man after all, forgot every other consideration, and no longer thought of aught save the happiness of feasting his eyes upon the charming spectacle which Candaules was about to offer him. One cannot demand from a captain of twenty-five the austerity of a hoary philosopher.

At last a low whispering of raiment sweeping and trailing over marble, distinctly audible in the deep silence of the night, announced the approach of the queen. In effect it was she. With a step as cadenced and rhythmic as an ode, she crossed the threshold of the thalamus, and the wind of her veil with its floating folds almost touched the burning cheek of Gyges, who felt wellnigh on the point of fainting, and found himself compelled to seek the support of the wall; but soon recovering from the violence of his emotions, he approached the chink of the door, and took the most favourable position for enabling him to lose nothing of the scene whereof he was about to be an invisible witness.

Nyssia advanced to the ivory chair and commenced to detach the pins, terminated by hollow balls of gold, which fastened her veil upon her head; and Gyges from the depths of the shadow-filled angle where he stood concealed could examine at his ease the proud and charming face of which he had before obtained only a hurried glimpse; that rounded neck, at once delicate and powerful, whereon Aphrodite had traced with the nail of her little finger those three faint lines which are still at this very day known as the 'necklace of Venus'; that white nape on whose alabaster surface little wild rebellious curls were disporting and entwining themselves; those silver shoulders, half rising from the opening of the chlamys, like the moon's disc emerging from an opaque cloud. Candaules, half reclining upon his cushions, gazed with fondness upon his wife, and thought to himself: 'Now Gyges, who is so cold, so difficult to please, and so sceptical, must be already half convinced.'

Opening a little coffer which stood on a table supported by one leg terminating in carven lion's paws, the queen freed her beautiful arms from the weight of the bracelets and jewellery wherewith they had been overburdened during the day—arms whose form and whiteness might well have enabled them to compare with those of Hera, sister and wife of Zeus, the lord of Olympus. Precious as were her jewels, they were assuredly not worth the spots which they concealed, and had Nyssia been a coquette, one might have well supposed that she only donned them in order that she should be entreated to take them off. The rings and chased work had left upon her skin, fine and tender as the interior pulp of a lily, light rosy imprints, which she soon dissipated by rubbing them with her little taper-fingered hand, all rounded and slender at its extremities.

Then with the movement of a dove trembling in the snow of its feathers, she shook her hair, which being no longer held by the golden pins, rolled down in languid spirals like hyacinth flowers over her back and bosom. Thus she remained for a few moments ere reassembling the scattered curls and finally re-uniting them into one mass. It was marvellous to watch the blond ringlets streaming like jets of liquid gold between the silver of her fingers; and her arms undulating like swans' necks as they were arched above her head in the act of twisting and confining the natural bullion. If you have ever by chance examined one of those beautiful Etruscan vases with red figures on a black ground, and decorated with one of those subjects which are designated under the title of 'Greek Toilette,' then you will have some idea of the grace of Nyssia in that attitude which, from the age of antiquity to our own era, has furnished such a multitude of happy designs for painters and statuaries.

Having thus arranged her coiffure, she seated herself upon the edge of the ivory footstool and commenced to untie the little bands which fastened her buskins. We moderns, owing to our horrible system of footgear, which is hardly less absurd than the Chinese shoe, no longer know what a foot is. That of Nyssia was of a perfection rare even in Greece and antique Asia. The great toe, a little apart like the thumb of a bird, the other toes, slightly long, and all ranged in charming symmetry, the nails well shaped and brilliant as agates, the ankles well rounded and supple, the heel slightly tinted with a rosy hue—nothing was wanting to the perfection of the little member. The leg attached to this foot, and which gleamed like polished marble under the lamp-light, was irreproachable in the purity of its outlines and the grace of its curves.

Gyges, lost in contemplation, though all the while fully comprehending the madness of Candaules, said to himself that had the gods bestowed such a treasure upon him he would have known how to keep it to himself.

'Well, Nyssia, are you not coming to sleep with me?' exclaimed Candaules, seeing that the queen was not hurrying herself in the least, and feeling desirous to abridge the watch of Gyges.

'Yes, my dear lord, I will soon be ready,' answered Nyssia.

And she detached the cameo which fastened the peplum upon her shoulder. There remained only the tunic to let fall. Gyges, behind the door, felt his veins hiss through his temples; his heart beat so violently that he feared it must make itself heard in the chamber, and to repress its fierce pulsations he pressed his hand upon his bosom; and when Nyssia, with a movement of careless grace, unfastened the girdle of her tunic, he thought his knees would give way beneath him.

Nyssia—was it an instinctive presentiment, or was her skin, virginally pure from profane looks, so delicately magnetic in its susceptibility that it could feel the rays of a passionate eye though that eye was invisible?—Nyssia hesitated to strip herself of that tunic, the last rampart of her modesty. Twice or thrice her shoulders, her bosom, and bare arms shuddered with a nervous chill, as though they had been suddenly grazed by the wings of a nocturnal butterfly, or as though an insolent lip had dared to touch them in the darkness.

At last, seeming to nerve herself for a sudden resolve she doffed the tunic in its turn; and the white poem of her divine body suddenly appeared in all its splendour, like the statue of a goddess unveiled on the day of a temple's inauguration. Shuddering with pleasure the light glided and gloated over those exquisite forms, and covered them with timid kisses, profiting by an occasion, alas, rare indeed! The rays scattered through the chamber, disdaining to illuminate golden arms, jewelled clasps, or brazen tripods, all concentrated themselves upon Nyssia, and left all other objects in obscurity. Were we Greeks of the age of Pericles we might at our ease eulogise those beautiful serpentine lines, those polished flanks, those elegant curves, those breasts which might have served as moulds for the cup of Hebe; but modern prudery forbids such descriptions, for the pen cannot find pardon for what is permitted to the chisel; and besides, there are some things which can be written of only in marble.

Candaules smiled in proud satisfaction. With a rapid step, as though ashamed of being so beautiful, for she was only the daughter of a man and a woman, Nyssia approached the bed, her arms folded upon her bosom; but with a sudden movement she turned round ere taking her place upon the couch beside her royal spouse, and beheld through the aperture of the door a gleaming eye flaming like the carbuncle of Oriental legend; for if it were false that she had a double pupil, and that she possessed the stone which is found in the heads of dragons, it was at least true that her green glance penetrated darkness like the glaucous eye of the cat and tiger.

A cry, like that of a fawn who receives an arrow in her flank while tranquilly dreaming among the leafy shadows, was on the point of bursting from her lips, yet she found strength to control herself, and lay down beside Candaules, cold as a serpent, with the violets of death upon her cheeks and lips. Not a muscle of her limbs quivered, not a fibre of her body palpitated, and soon her slow, regular breathing seemed to indicate that Morpheus had distilled his poppy juice upon her eyelids.

She had divined and comprehended all.

CHAPTER IV

Gyges, trembling and distracted with passion, had retired, following exactly the instructions of Candaules; and if Nyssia, through some unfortunate chance, had not turned her head ere taking her place upon the couch, and perceived him in the act of taking flight, doubtless she would have remained for ever unconscious of the outrage done to her charms by a husband more passionate than scrupulous.

Accustomed to the winding corridors of the palace, the young warrior had no difficulty in finding his way out. He passed through the city at a reckless pace like a madman escaped from Anticyra, and by making himself known to the sentinels who guarded the ramparts, he had the gates opened for him and gained the fields beyond. His brain burned, his cheeks flamed as with the fires of fever; his breath came hotly panting through his lips; he flung himself down upon the meadow-sod humid with the tears of the night; and at last hearing in the darkness, through the thick grass and water-plants, the silvery respiration of a Naiad, he dragged himself to the spring, plunged his hands and arms into the crystal flood, bathed his face, and drank several mouthfuls of the water in the hope to cool the ardour which was devouring him. Any one who could have seen him thus hopelessly bending over the spring in the feeble starlight would have taken him for Narcissus pursuing his own shadow; but it was not of himself assuredly that Gyges was enamoured.

The rapid apparition of Nyssia had dazzled his eyes like the keen zigzag of a lightning flash. He beheld her floating before him in a luminous whirlwind, and felt that never through all his life could he banish that image from his vision. His love had grown to vastness; its flower had suddenly burst, like those plants which open their blossoms with a clap of thunder. To master his passion were henceforth a thing impossible: as well counsel the empurpled waves which Poseidon lifts with his trident to lie tranquilly in their bed of sand and cease to foam upon the rocks of the shore. Gyges was no longer master of himself, and he felt a miserable despair, as of a man riding in a chariot, who finds his terrified and uncontrollable horses rushing with all the speed of a furious gallop toward some rock-bristling precipice. A hundred thousand projects, each wilder than the last, whirled confusedly through his brain. He blasphemed Destiny, he cursed his mother for having given him life, and the gods that they had not caused him to be born to a throne, for then he might have been able to espouse the daughter of the satrap.

A frightful agony gnawed at his heart; he was jealous of the king. From the moment of the tunic's fall at the feet of Nyssia, like the flight of a white dove alighting upon a meadow, it had seemed to him that she belonged to him; he deemed himself despoiled of his wealth by Candaules. In all his amorous reveries he had never until then thought of the husband; he had thought of the queen only as of a pure abstraction, without representing to himself in fancy all those intimate details of conjugal familiarity, so poignant, so bitter for those who love a woman in the power of another. Now he had beheld Nyssia's blond head bending like a blossom beside the dark head of Candaules. The very thought of it had inflamed his anger to the highest degree, although a moment's reflection should have convinced him that things could not have come to pass otherwise, and he felt growing within him a most unjust hatred against his master. The act of having compelled his presence at the queen's dishabille seemed to him a barbarous irony, an odious refinement of cruelty, for he did not remember that his love for her could not have been known by the king, who had sought in him only a confidant of easy morals and a connoisseur in beauty. That which he ought to have regarded as a great favour affected him like a mortal injury for which he was meditating vengeance. While thinking that tomorrow the same scene of which he had been a mute and invisible witness would infallibly renew itself, his tongue clove to his palate, his forehead became imbeaded with drops of cold sweat, and his hand convulsively grasped the hilt of his great double-edged sword.

Nevertheless, thanks to the freshness of the night, that excellent counsellor, he became a little calmer, and returned to

Sardes before the morning light had become bright enough to enable a few early rising citizens and slaves to notice the pallor of his brow and the disorder of his apparel. He betook himself to his regular post at the palace, well suspecting that Can-daules would shortly send for him; and, however violent the agitation of his feelings, he felt he was not powerful enough to brave the anger of the king, and could in no way escape submitting again to this rôle of confidant, which could thenceforth only inspire him with horror. Having arrived at the palace, he seated himself upon the steps of the cypress-panelled vestibule, leaned his back against a column, and, under the pretext of being fatigued by the long vigil under arms, he covered his head with his mantle and feigned sleep, to avoid answering the questions of the other guards.

If the night had been terrible to Gyges, it had not been less so to Nyssia, as she never for an instant doubted that he had been purposely hidden there by Candaules. The king's persistency in begging her not to veil so austerely a face which the gods had made for the admiration of men, his evident vexation upon her refusal to appear in Greek costume at the sacrifices and public solemnities, his unsparing raillery at what he termed her barbarian shyness, all tended to convince her that the young Heracleid had sought to admit some one into those mysteries which should remain secret to all, for without his encouragement no man could have dared to risk himself in an undertaking the discovery of which would have resulted in the punishment of a speedy death.

How slowly did the black hours seem to her to pass! How anxiously did she await the coming of dawn to mingle its bluish tints with the yellow gleams of the almost exhausted lamp! It seemed to her that Apollo would never mount his chariot again, and that some invisible hand was sustaining the sand of the hourglass in air. Though brief as any other, that night seemed to her like the Cimmerian nights, six long months of darkness.

While it lasted she lay motionless and rigid at full length on the very edge of her couch in dread of being touched by Candaules. If she had not up to that night felt a very strong love for the son of Myrsus, she had, at least, ever exhibited toward him that grave and serene tenderness which every virtuous woman entertains for her husband, although the altogether Greek freedom of his morals frequently displeased her, and though he entertained ideas at variance with her own in regard to modesty; but after such an affront she could only feel the chilliest hatred and most icy contempt for him; she would have preferred even death to one of his caresses. Such an outrage it was impossible to forgive, for among the barbarians, and above all among the Persians and Bactrians, it was held a great disgrace, not for women only, but even for men, to be seen without their garments.

At length Candaules arose, and Nyssia, awaking from her simulated sleep, hurried from that chamber now profaned in her eyes as though it had served for the nocturnal orgies of Bacchantes and courtesans. It was agony for her to breathe that impure air any longer, and that she might freely give herself up to her grief she took refuge in the upper apartments reserved for the women, summoned her slaves by clapping her hands, and poured ewers of water over her shoulders, her bosom, and her whole body, as though hoping by this species of lustral ablution to efface the soil imprinted by the eyes of Gyges. She would have voluntarily torn, as it were, from her body that skin upon which the rays shot from a burning pupil seemed to have left their traces. Taking from the hands of her waiting-women the thick downy materials which served to drink up the last pearls of the bath, she wiped herself with such violence that a slight purple cloud rose to the spots she had rubbed.

'In vain,' she exclaimed, letting the damp tissues fall, and dismissing her attendants—'in vain would I pour over myself all the waters of all the springs and the rivers; the ocean with all its bitter gulfs could not purify me. Such a stain may be washed out only with blood. Oh, that look, that look! It has incrusted itself upon me; it clasps me, covers me, burns me like the tunic dipped in the blood of Nessus; I feel it beneath my draperies, like an envenomed tissue which nothing can detach from my body! Now, indeed, would I vainly pile garments upon garments, select materials the least transparent, and the thickest of mantles. I would none the less bear upon my naked flesh this infamous robe woven by one adulterous and lascivious glance. Vainly, since the hour when I issued from the chaste womb of my mother, have I been brought up in private, enveloped, like Isis, the Egyptian goddess, with a veil of which none might have lifted the hem without paying for his audacity with his life. In vain have I remained guarded from all evil desires, from all profane imaginings, unknown of men, virgin as the snow on which the eagle himself could not imprint the seal of his talons, so loftily does the mountain which it covers lift its head in the pure and icy air. The depraved caprice of a Lydian Greek has sufficed to make me lose in a single instant, without any guilt of mine, all the fruit of long years of precaution and reserve. Innocent and dishonoured, hidden from all yet made public to all . . . this is the lot to which Candaules has condemned me. Who can assure me that, at this very moment, Gyges is not in the act of discoursing upon my charms with some soldiers at the very threshold of the palace? Oh shame! Oh infamy! Two men have beheld me naked and yet at this instant enjoy the sweet light of the sun! In what does Nyssia now differ from the most shameless hetaira, from the vilest of courtesans? This body which I have striven to render worthy of being the habitation of a pure and noble soul, serves for a theme of conversation; it is talked of like some lascivious idol brought from Sicyon or from Corinth; it is commended or found fault with. The shoulder is perfect, the arm is charming, perhaps a little thin—what know I? All the blood of my heart leaps to my cheeks at such a thought. Oh beauty, fatal gift of the gods! why am I not the wife of some poor mountain goatherd of innocent and simple habits? He would not have suborned a goatherd like himself at the threshold of his cabin to profane his humble happiness! My lean figure, my unkempt hair, my complexion faded by the burning sun, would then have saved me from so gross an insult, and my honest homeliness would not have been compelled to blush. How shall I dare, after the scene of this night, to pass before those men, proudly erect under the folds of a tunic which has no longer aught to hide from either of them. I should drop dead with shame upon the pavement. Candaules, Candaules, I was at least entitled to more respect from you, and there was nothing in my conduct which could have provoked such an outrage. Was I one of those ones whose arms for ever cling like ivy to their husbands' necks, and who seem more like slaves bought with money for a master's pleasure than free-born women of noble blood? Have I ever after a repast sung amorous hymns accompanying myself upon the lyre, with wine-moist lips, naked shoulders, and a wreath of roses about my hair, or given you cause, by any immodest action, to treat me like a mistress whom one shows after a banquet to his companions in debauch?' While

Nyssia was thus buried in her grief, great tears overflowed from her eyes like rain-drops from the azure chalice of a lotus-flower after some storm, and rolling down her pale cheeks fell upon her fair forlorn hands, languishingly open, like roses whose leaves are half-shed, for no order came from the brain to give them activity. The attitude of Niobe, beholding her fourteenth child succumb beneath the arrows of Apollo and Diana, was not more sadly despairing, but soon starting from this state of prostration, she rolled herself upon the floor, rent her garments, covered her beautiful dishevelled hair with ashes, tore her bosom and cheeks with her nails amid convulsive sobs, and abandoned herself to all the excesses of Oriental grief, the more violently that she had been forced so long to contain her indignation, shame, pangs of wounded dignity, and all the agony that convulsed her soul, for the pride of her whole life had been broken, and the idea that she had nothing wherewith to reproach herself afforded her no consolation. As a poet has said, only the innocent know remorse. She was repenting of the crime which another had committed.

Nevertheless she made an effort to recover herself, ordered the baskets filled with wools of different colours, and the spindles wrapped with flax, to be brought to her, and distributed the work to her women as she had been accustomed to do; but she thought she noticed that the slaves looked at her in a very peculiar way, and had ceased to entertain the same timid respect for her as before. Her voice no longer rang with the same assurance; there was something humble and furtive in her demeanour; she felt herself interiorly fallen.

Doubtless her scruples were exaggerated, and her virtue had received no stain from the folly of Candaules; but ideas imbibed with a mother's milk obtain irresistible sway, and the modesty of the body is carried by Oriental nations to an extent almost incomprehensible to Occidental races. When a man desired to speak to Nyssia in the palace of Megabazus at Bactria, he was obliged to do so keeping his eyes fixed upon the ground, and two eunuchs stood beside him, poniard in hand, ready to plunge their keen blades through his heart should he dare lift his head to look at the princess, notwithstanding that her face was veiled. You may readily conceive, therefore, how deadly an injury the action of Candaules would seem to a woman thus brought up, while any other would doubtless have considered it only a culpable frivolity. Thus the idea of vengeance had instantly presented itself to Nyssia, and had given her sufficient self-control to strangle the cry of her offended modesty ere it reached her lips, at the moment when, turning her head, she beheld the burning eyes of Gyges flaming through the darkness. She must have possessed the courage of the warrior in ambush, who, wounded by a random dart, utters no syllable of pain through fear of betraying himself behind his shelter of foliage or river-reeds, and in silence permits his blood to stripe his flesh with long red lines. Had she not withheld that first impulse to cry aloud, Candaules, alarmed and forewarned, would have kept upon his guard, which must have rendered it more difficult, if not impossible, to carry out her purpose.

Nevertheless, as yet she had conceived no definite plan, but she had resolved that the insult done to her honour should be fully expiated. At first she had thought of killing Candaules herself while he slept, with the sword hung at the bedside. But she recoiled from the thought of dipping her beautiful hands in blood; she feared lest she might miss her blow; and, with all her bitter anger, she hesitated at so violent and unwomanly an act.

Suddenly she appeared to have decided upon some project. She summoned Statira, one of the waiting-women who had come with her from Bactria, and in whom she placed much confidence, and whispered a few words close to her ear in a very low voice, although there were no other persons in the room, as if she feared that even the walls might hear her.

Statira bowed low, and immediately left the apartment.

Like all persons who are actually menaced by some great peril, Candaules presumed himself perfectly secure. He was certain that Gyges had stolen away unperceived, and he thought only upon the delight of conversing with him about the unrivalled attractions of his wife.

So he caused him to be summoned, and conducted him to the Court of the Heracleidæ.

'Well, Gyges,' he said to him with laughing mien, 'I did not deceive you when I assured you that you would not regret having passed a few hours behind that blessed door. Am I right? Do you know of any living woman more beautiful than the queen? If you know of any superior to her, tell me so frankly, and go bear her in my name this string of pearls, the symbol of power.'

'Sire,' replied Gyges in a voice trembling with emotion, 'no human creature is worthy to compare with Nyssia. It is not the pearl fillet of queens which should adorn her brows, but only the starry crown of the immortals.'

'I well knew that your ice must melt at last in the fires of that sun. Now can you comprehend my passion, my delirium, my mad desires? Is it not true, Gyges, that the heart of a man is not great enough to contain such a love? It must overflow and diffuse itself.'

A hot blush overspread the cheeks of Gyges, who now but too well comprehended the admiration of Candaules.

The king noticed it, and said, with a manner half smiling, half serious:

'My poor friend, do not commit the folly of becoming enamoured of Nyssia; you would lose your pains. It is a statue which I have enabled you to see, not a woman. I have allowed you to read some stanzas of a beautiful poem, whereof I alone possess the manuscript, merely for the purpose of having your opinion; that is all.'

'You have no need, sire, to remind me of my nothingness. Sometimes the humblest slave is visited in his slumbers by some radiant and lovely vision, with ideal forms, nacreous flesh, ambrosial hair. I—I have dreamed with open eyes; you are the god who sent me that dream.'

'Now,' continued the king, 'it will scarcely be necessary for me to enjoin silence upon you. If you do not keep a seal upon your lips you might learn to your cost that Nyssia is not as good as she is beautiful.'

The king waved his hand in token of farewell to his confidant, and retired for the purpose of inspecting an antique bed sculptured by Ikmalius, a celebrated artisan, which had been offered him for purchase.

Candaules had scarcely disappeared when a woman, wrapped in a long mantle so as to leave but one of her eyes exposed, after the fashion of the barbarians, came forth from the shadow of a column behind which she had kept herself hidden during the conversation of the king and his favourite, walked straight to Gyges, placed her finger upon his shoulder, and made a sign to him to follow her.

CHAPTER V

Statira, followed by Gyges, paused before a little door, of which she raised the latch by pulling a silver ring attached to a leathern strap, and commenced to ascend a stairway with rather high steps contrived in the thickness of the wall. At the head of the stairway was a second door, which she opened with a key wrought of ivory and brass. As soon as Gyges entered she disappeared without any further explanation in regard to what was expected of him.

The curiosity of Gyges was mingled with uneasiness. He could form no idea as to the significance of this mysterious message. He had a vague fancy that he could recognise in the silent Iris one of Nyssia's women; and the way by which she had made him follow her led to the queen's apartments. He asked himself in terror whether he had been perceived in his hiding-place or betrayed by Candaules, for both suppositions seemed probable.

At the idea that Nyssia knew all, he felt his face bedewed with a sweat alternately burning and icy. He sought to fly, but the door had been fastened upon him by Statira, and all escape was cut off; then he advanced into the chamber, which was shadowed by heavy purple hangings, and found himself face to face with Nyssia. He thought he beheld a statue rise before him, such was her pallor. The hues of life had abandoned her face; a feeble rose tint alone animated her lips; on her tender temples a few almost imperceptible veins intercrossed their azure network; tears had swollen her eyelids, and left shining furrows upon the down of her cheeks; the chrysoprase tints of her eyes had lost their intensity. She was even more beautiful and touching thus. Sorrow had given soul to her marmorean beauty.

Her disordered robe, scarcely fastened to her shoulders, left visible her beautiful bare arms, her throat, and the commencement of her death-white bosom. Like a warrior vanquished in his first conflict, her beauty had laid down its arms. Of what use to her would have been the draperies which conceal form, the tunics with their carefully fastened folds? Did not Gyges know her? Wherefore defend what has been lost in advance?

She walked straight to Gyges, and fixing upon him an imperial look, clear and commanding, said to him in a quick, abrupt voice:

'Do not lie; seek no vain subterfuges; have at least the dignity and courage of your crime. I know all; I saw you! Not a word of excuse. I would not listen to it. Candaules himself concealed you behind the door. Is it not so the thing happened? And you fancy, doubtless, that it is all over? Unhappily I am not a Greek woman, pliant to the whims of artists and voluptuaries. Nyssia will not serve for any one's toy. There are now two men, one of whom is a man too much upon the earth. He must disappear from it! Unless he dies, I cannot live. It will be either you or Candaules. I leave you master of the choice. Kill him, avenge me, and win by that murder both my hand and the throne of Lydia, or else shall a prompt death henceforth prevent you from beholding, through a cowardly complaisance, what you have not the right to look upon. He who commanded is more culpable than he who has only obeyed; and, moreover, should you become my husband, no one will have ever seen me without having the right to do so. But make your decision at once, for two of those four eyes in which my nudity has reflected itself must before this very evening be for ever extinguished.'

This strange alternative, proposed with a terrible coolness, with an immutable resolution, so utterly surprised Gyges, who was expecting reproaches, menaces, and a violent scene, that he remained for several minutes without colour and without voice, livid as a shade on the shores of the black rivers of hell.

'I! to dip my hands in the blood of my master! Is it indeed you, O queen, who demand of me so great a penalty? I comprehend all your anger, I feel it to be just, and it was not my fault that this outrage took place; but you know that kings are mighty, they descend from a divine race. Our destinies repose on their august knees; and it is not we, feeble mortals, who may hesitate at their commands. Their will overthrows our refusal, as a dyke is swept away by a torrent By your feet that I kiss, by the hem of your robe which I touch as a suppliant, be clement! Forget this injury, which is known to none, and which shall remain eternally buried in darkness and silence!

Candaules worships you, admires you, and his fault springs only from an excess of love.'

'Were you addressing a sphinx of granite in the arid sands of Egypt, you would have more chance of melting her. The winged words might fly uninterruptedly from your lips for a whole Olympiad; you could not move my resolution in the slightest. A heart of brass dwells in this marble breast of mine. Die or kill! When the sunbeam which has passed through the curtains shall touch the foot of this table let your choice have been made. I wait.'

And Nyssia crossed her arms upon her breast in an attitude replete with sombre majesty.

To behold her standing erect, motionless and pale, her eyes fixed, her brows contracted, her hair in disorder, her foot firmly placed upon the pavement, one would have taken her for Nemesis descended from her griffin, and awaiting the hour to smite a guilty one.

'The shadowy depths of Hades are visited by none with pleasure,' answered Gyges. 'It is sweet to enjoy the pure light of day; and the heroes themselves who dwell in the Fortunate Isles would gladly return to their native land. Each man has the instinct of self-preservation, and since blood must flow, let it be rather from the veins of another than from mine.'

To these sentiments, avowed by Gyges with antique frankness, were added others more noble whereof he did not speak. He was desperately in love with Nyssia and jealous of Candaules. It was not, therefore, the fear of death alone that had induced him to undertake this bloody task. The thought of leaving Candaules in free possession of Nyssia was insupportable to him: and, moreover, the vertigo of fatality had seized him. By a succession of irregular and terrible events he beheld himself hurried toward the realisation of his dreams; a mighty wave had lifted him and borne him on in despite of his efforts; Nyssia herself was extending her hand to him, to help him to ascend the steps of the royal throne. All this had caused him to forget that Candaules was his master and his benefactor; for none can flee from Fate, and Necessity walks on with nails in one hand and whip in the other, to stop your advance or to urge you forward.

'It is well,' replied Nyssia; 'here is the means of execution.' And she drew from her bosom a Bactrian poniard, with a jade handle enriched with inlaid circles of white gold. 'This blade is not made of brass, but with iron difficult to work, tempered in flame and water, so that Hephaistos himself could not forge one more keenly pointed or finely edged. It would pierce, like thin papyrus, metal cuirasses and bucklers of dragon's skin.

'The time,' she continued, with the same icy coolness, 'shall be while he slumbers. Let him sleep and wake no more!'

Her accomplice, Gyges, hearkened to her words with stupefaction, for he had never thought he could find such resolution in a woman who could not bring herself to lift her veil.

'The ambuscade shall be laid in the very same place where the infamous one concealed you in order to expose me to your gaze. At the approach of night I shall turn back one of the folding-doors upon you, undress myself, lie down, and when he shall be asleep I will give you a signal. Above all things, let there be no hesitancy, no feebleness; and take heed that your hand does not tremble when the moment shall have come! And now, for fear lest you might change your mind, I propose to make sure of your person until the fatal hour. You might attempt to escape, to forewarn your master. Do not think to do so.'

Nyssia whistled in a peculiar way, and immediately from behind a Persian tapestry embroidered with flowers, there appeared four monsters, swarthy, clad in robes diagonally striped, which left visible arms muscled and gnarled as trunks of oaks. Their thick pouting lips, the gold rings which they wore through the partition of their nostrils, their great teeth sharp as the fangs of wolves, the expression of stupid servility on their faces, rendered them hideous to behold.

The queen pronounced some words in a language unknown to Gyges, doubtless in Bactrian, and the four slaves rushed upon the young man, seized him, and carried him away, even as a nurse might carry off a child in the fold of her robe.

Now, what were Nyssia's real thoughts? Had she, indeed, noticed Gyges at the time of her meeting with him near Bactria, and preserved some memory of the young captain in one of those secret recesses of the heart where even the most virtuous women always have something buried? Was the desire to avenge her modesty goaded by some other unacknowledged desire? And if Gyges had not been the handsomest young man in all Asia would she have evinced the same ardour in punishing Candaules for having outraged the sanctity of marriage? That is a delicate question to resolve, especially after a lapse of three thousand years; and although we have consulted Herodotus, Hephæstion, Plato, Dositheus, Archilochus of Paros, Hesychius of Miletus, Ptolomæus, Euphorion, and all who have spoken either at length or in only a few words concerning Candaules, Nyssia, and Gyges, we have been unable to arrive at any definite conclusion. To pursue so fleeting a shadow through so many centuries, under the ruins of so many crumpled empires, under the dust of departed nations, is a work of extreme difficulty, not to say impossibility.

At all events, Nyssia's resolution was implacably taken; this murder appeared to her in the light of the accomplishment of a sacred duty. Among the barbarian nations every man who has surprised a woman in her nakedness is put to death. The queen believed herself exercising her right; only inasmuch as the injury had been secret, she was doing herself justice as best she could. The passive accomplice would become the executioner of the other, and the punishment would thus spring from the crime itself. The hand would chastise the head.

The olive-tinted monsters shut Gyges up in an obscure portion of the palace, whence it was impossible that he could escape, or that his cries could be heard.

He passed the remainder of the day there in a state of cruel anxiety, accusing the hours of being lame, and again of walking too speedily. The crime which he was about to commit, although he was only, in some sort, the instrument of it, and though he was only yielding to an irresistible influence, presented itself to his mind in the most sombre colours. If the blow should miss through one of those circumstances which none could foresee? If the people of Sardes should revolt and seek to avenge the death of the king? Such were the very sensible though useless reflections which Gyges made while waiting to be taken from his prison and led to the place whence he could only depart to strike his master.

At last the night unfolded her starry robe in the sky, and its shadow fell upon the city and the palace. A light footstep became audible, a veiled woman entered the room and conducted him through the obscure corridors and multiplied mazes of the royal edifice with as much confidence as though she had been preceded by a slave bearing a lamp or a torch.

The hand which held that of Gyges was cold, soft, and small; nevertheless those slender fingers clasped it with a bruising force, as the fingers of some statue of brass animated by a prodigy would have done. The rigidity of an inflexible will betrayed itself in that ever-equal pressure as of a vice—a pressure which no hesitation of head or heart came to vary. Gyges, conquered, subjugated, crushed, yielded to that imperious traction, as though he were borne along by the mighty arm of Fate.

Alas! it was not thus he had wished to touch for the first time that fair royal hand, which had presented the poniard to him, and was leading him to murder, for it was Nyssia herself who had come for Gyges, to conceal him in the place of ambuscade.

No word was exchanged between the sinister couple on the way from the prison to the nuptial chamber.

The queen unfastened the thongs, raised the bar of the entrance, and placed Gyges behind the folding-door as Candaules had done the evening previous. This repetition of the same acts, with so different a purpose, had something of a lugubrious and fatal character. Vengeance, this time, had placed her foot upon every track left by the insult. The chastisement and the crime alike followed the same path. Yesterday it was the turn of Candaules, today it was that of Nyssia; and Gyges, accomplice in the injury, was also accomplice in the penalty. He had served the king to dishonour the queen; he would serve the queen to kill the king, equally exposed by the vices of the one and the virtues of the other.

The daughter of Megabazus seemed to feel a savage joy, a ferocious pleasure, in employing only the same means chosen by the Lydian king, and turning to account for the murder those very precautions which had been adopted for voluptuous fantasy.

'You will again this evening see me take off these garments which are so displeasing to Candaules. This spectacle should become wearisome to you,' said the queen in accents of bitter irony, as she stood on the threshold of the chamber; 'you will end by finding me ugly.' And a sardonic, forced laugh momentarily curled her pale mouth; then, regaining her impassible severity of mien, she continued: 'Do not imagine you will be able to steal away this time as you did before; you know my sight is piercing. At the slightest movement on your part I shall awake Candaules; and you know that it will not be easy for you to explain what you are doing in the king's apartments, behind a door, with a poniard in your hand. Further, my Bactrian slaves, the copper-coloured mutes who imprisoned you a short time ago, guard all the issues of the palace, with orders to massacre you should you attempt to go out. Therefore let no vain scruples of fidelity cause you to hesitate. Think that I will make you King of Sardes, and that . . . I will love you if you avenge me. The blood of Candaules will be your purple, and his death will make for you a place in that bed.'

The slaves came according to their custom to change the fuel in the tripod, renew the oil in the lamps, spread tapestry and the skins of animals upon the royal couch; and Nyssia hurried into the chamber as soon as she heard their footsteps resounding in the distance.

In a short time Candaules arrived all joyous. He had purchased the bed of Ikmalius and proposed to substitute it for the bed wrought after the Oriental fashion, which he declared had never been much to his taste. He seemed pleased to find that Nyssia had already retired to the nuptial chamber.

'The trade of embroidery, and spindles, and needles seems not to have the same attraction for you today as usual. In fact, it is a monotonous labour to perpetually pass one thread between other threads, and I wonder at the pleasure which you seem ordinarily to take in it. To tell the truth, I am afraid that some fine day Pallas-Athene, on finding you so skilful, will break her shuttle over your head as she once did to poor Arachne.'

'My lord, I felt somewhat tired this evening, and so came downstairs sooner than usual. Would you not like before going to sleep to drink a cup of black Samian wine mixed with the honey of Hymettus?' And she poured from a golden urn, into a cup of the same metal, the sombre-coloured beverage which she had mingled with the soporiferous juice of the nepenthe.

Candaules took the cup by both handles and drained it to the last drop; but the young Heracleid had a strong head, and sinking his elbow into the cushions of his couch he watched Nyssia undressing without any sign that the dust of sleep was commencing to gather upon his eyes.

As on the evening before, Nyssia unfastened her hair and permitted its rich blond waves to ripple over her shoulders. From his hiding-place Gyges fancied that he saw those locks slowly becoming suffused with tawny tints, illuminated with reflections of blood and flame; and their heavy curls seemed to lengthen with vipérine undulations, like the hair of the Gorgons and Medusas.

All simple and graceful as that action was in itself, it took from the terrible events about to transpire a frightful and ominous character, which caused the hidden assassin to shudder with terror.

Nyssia then unfastened her bracelets, but agitated as her hands had been by nervous straining, they ill served her will. She broke the string of a bracelet of beads of amber inlaid with gold, which rolled over the floor with a loud noise, causing Candaules to reopen his gradually closing eyes.

Each one of those beads fell upon the heart of Gyges as a drop of molten lead falls upon water.

Having unlaced her buskins, the queen threw her upper tunic over the back of an ivory chair. This drapery, thus arranged, produced upon Gyges the effect of one of those sinister-folding winding-sheets wherein the dead were wrapped ere being borne to the funeral pyre. Every object in that room, which had the evening before seemed to him one scene of smiling splendour, now appeared to him livid, dim, and menacing. The statues of basalt rolled their eyes and smiled hideously. The lamp flickered weirdly, and its flame dishevelled itself in red and sanguine rays like the crest of a comet. Far back in the dimly lighted corners loomed the monstrous forms of the Lares and Lémures. The mantles hanging from their hooks seemed animated by a factitious life, and assumed a human aspect of vitality; and when Nyssia stripped of her last garment, approached the bed, all white and naked as a shade, he thought that Death herself had broken the diamond fetters wherewith Hercules of old enchained her at the gates of hell when he delivered Alcestes, and had come in person to take possession of Candaules.

Overcome by the power of the nepenthe-juice, the king at last slumbered. Nyssia made a sign for Gyges to come forth from his retreat; and laying her finger upon the breast of the victim, she directed upon her accomplice a look so humid, so lustrous, so weighty with languishment, so replete with intoxicating promise, that Gyges, maddened and fascinated, sprang from his hiding-place like the tiger from the summit of the rock where it has been couching, traversed the chamber at a bound, and plunged the Bactrian poniard up to the very hilt in the heart of the descendant of Hercules. The chastity of Nyssia was avenged, and the dream of Gyges accomplished.

Thus ended the dynasty of the Heracleidæ, after having endured for five hundred and five years, and commenced that of the Mermnades in the person of Gyges, son of Dascylus. The Sardians, indignant at the death of Candaules, threatened revolt; but the oracle of Delphi having declared in favour of Gyges, who had sent thither a vast number of silver vases and six golden cratera of the value of thirty talents, the new king maintained his seat on the throne of Lydia, which he occupied for many long years, lived happily, and never showed his wife to any one, knowing too well what it cost. one, knowing too well what it cost.

CLARIMONDE

Brother, you ask me if I have ever loved. Yes. My story is a strange and terrible one; and though I am sixty-six years of age, I scarcely dare even now to disturb the ashes of that memory. To you I can refuse nothing; but I should not relate such a tale to any less experienced mind. So strange were the circumstances of my story, that I can scarcely believe myself to have ever actually been a party to them. For more than three years I remained the victim of a most singular and diabolical illusion. Poor country priest though I was, I led every night in a dream—would to God it had been all a dream!—a most worldly life, a damning life, a life of Sardanapalus. One single look too freely cast upon a woman well-nigh caused me to lose my soul; but finally by the grace of God and the assistance of my patron saint, I succeeded in casting out the evil spirit that possessed me. My daily life was long interwoven with a nocturnal life of a totally different character. By day I was a priest of the Lord, occupied with prayer and sacred things; by night, from the instant that I closed my eyes I became a young nobleman, a fine connoisseur in women, dogs, and horses; gambling, drinking, and blaspheming; and when I awoke at early daybreak, it seemed to me, on the other hand, that I had been sleeping, and had only dreamed that I was a priest. Of this somnambulistic life there now remains to me only the recollection of certain scenes and words which I cannot banish from my memory; but although I never actually left the walls of my presbytery, one would think to hear me speak that I were a man who, weary of all worldly pleasures, had become a religious, seeking to end a tempestuous life in the service of God, rather than a humble seminarist who has grown old in this obscure curacy, situated in the depths of the woods and even isolated from the life of the century.

Yes, I have loved as none in the world ever loved—with an insensate and furious passion—so violent that I am astonished it did not cause my heart to burst asunder. Ah, what nights—what nights!

From my earliest childhood I had felt a vocation to the priesthood, so that all my studies were directed with that idea in view. Up to the age of twenty-four my life had been only a prolonged novitiate. Having completed my course of theology I successively received all the minor orders, and my superiors judged me worthy, despite my youth, to pass the last awful degree. My ordination was fixed for Easter week.

I had never gone into the world. My world was confined by the walls of the college and the seminary. I knew in a vague sort of a way that there was something called Woman, but I never permitted my thoughts to dwell on such a subject, and I lived in a state of perfect innocence. Twice a year only I saw my infirm and aged mother, and in those visits were comprised my sole relations with the outer world.

I regretted nothing; I felt not the least hesitation at taking the last irrevocable step; I was filled with joy and impatience. Never did a betrothed lover count the slow hours with more feverish ardour; I slept only to dream that I was saying mass; I believed there could be nothing in the world more delightful than to be a priest; I would have refused to be a king or a poet in preference. My ambition could conceive of no loftier aim.

I tell you this in order to show you that what happened to me could not have happened in the natural order of things, and to enable you to understand that I was the victim of an inexplicable fascination.

At last the great day came. I walked to the church with a step so light that I fancied myself sustained in air, or that I had wings upon my shoulders. I believed myself an angel, and wondered at the sombre and thoughtful faces of my companions, for there were several of us. I had passed all the night in prayer, and was in a condition wellnigh bordering on ecstasy. The bishop, a venerable old man, seemed to me God the Father leaning over His Eternity, and I beheld Heaven through the vault of the temple.

You well know the details of that ceremony—the benediction, the communion under both forms, the anointing of the palms of the hands with the Oil of Catechumens, and then the holy sacrifice offered in concert with the bishop.

Ah, truly spake Job when he declared that the imprudent man is one who hath not made a covenant with his eyes! I accidentally lifted my head, which until then I had kept down, and beheld before me, so close that it seemed that I could have touched her—although she was actually a considerable distance from me and on the further side of the sanctuary railing—a young woman of extraordinary beauty, and attired with royal magnificence. It seemed as though scales had suddenly fallen from my eyes. I felt like a blind man who unexpectedly recovers his sight. The bishop, so radiantly glorious but an instant before, suddenly vanished away, the tapers paled upon their golden candlesticks like stars in the dawn, and a vast darkness seemed to fill the whole church. The charming creature appeared in bright relief against the background of that darkness, like some angelic revelation. She seemed herself radiant, and radiating light rather than receiving it.

I lowered my eyelids, firmly resolved not to again open them, that I might not be influenced by external objects, for distraction had gradually taken possession of me until I hardly knew what I was doing.

In another minute, nevertheless, I reopened my eyes, for through my eyelashes I still beheld her, all sparkling with prismatic colours, and surrounded with such a penumbra as one beholds in gazing at the sun.

Oh, how beautiful she was! The greatest painters, who followed ideal beauty into heaven itself, and thence brought back to earth the true portrait of the Madonna, never in their delineations even approached that wildly beautiful reality which I saw before me. Neither the verses of the poet nor the palette of the artist could convey any conception of her. She was rather tall, with a form and bearing of a goddess. Her hair, of a soft blonde hue, was parted in the midst and flowed back over her temples in two rivers of rippling gold; she seemed a diademed queen. Her forehead, bluish-white in its transparency, extended its calm breadth above the arches of her eyebrows, which by a strange singularity were almost black, and admirably relieved the effect of sea-green eyes of unsustainable vivacity and brilliancy. What eyes! With a single flash they could have decided a man's destiny. They had a life, a limpidity, an ardour, a humid light which I have never seen in human eyes; they shot forth rays like arrows, which I could distinctly *see* enter my heart. I know not if the fire which illumined them came from heaven or from hell, but assuredly it came from one or the other. That woman was either an angel or a demon, perhaps both. Assuredly she never sprang from the flank of Eve, our common mother. Teeth of the most lustrous pearl gleamed in her ruddy smile, and at every inflection of her lips little dimples appeared in the satiny rose of her adorable cheeks. There was a delicacy and pride in the regal outline of her nostrils bespeaking noble blood. Agate gleams played over the smooth lustrous skin of her half-bare shoulders, and strings of great blonde pearls—almost equal to her neck in beauty of colour—descended upon her bosom. From time to time she elevated her head with the undulating grace of a startled serpent or peacock, thereby imparting a quivering motion to the high lace ruff which surrounded it like a silver trellis-work.

She wore a robe of orange-red velvet, and from her wide ermine-lined sleeves there peeped forth patrician hands of infinite delicacy, and so ideally transparent that, like the fingers of Aurora, they permitted the light to shine through them.

All these details I can recollect at this moment as plainly as though they were of yesterday, for notwithstanding I was greatly troubled at the time, nothing escaped me; the faintest touch of shading, the little dark speck at the point of the chin, the imperceptible down at the corners of the lips, the velvety floss upon the brow, the quivering shadows of the eyelashes upon the cheeks—I could notice everything with astonishing lucidity of perception.

And gazing I felt opening within me gates that had until then remained closed; vents long obstructed became all clear, permitting glimpses of unfamiliar perspectives within; life suddenly made itself visible to me under a totally novel aspect. I felt as though I had just been born into a new world and a new order of things. A frightful anguish commenced to torture-my heart as with red-hot pincers. Every successive minute seemed to me at once but a second and yet a century. Meanwhile the ceremony was proceeding, and I shortly found myself transported far from that world of which my newly born desires were furiously besieging the entrance. Nevertheless I answered 'Yes' when I wished to say 'No,' though all within me protested against the violence done to my soul by my tongue. Some occult power seemed to force the words from my throat against my will. Thus it is, perhaps, that so many young girls walk to the altar firmly resolved to refuse in a startling manner the husband imposed upon them, and that yet not one ever fulfils her intention. Thus it is, doubtless, that so many poor novices take the veil, though they have resolved to tear it into shreds at the moment when called upon to utter the vows. One dares not thus cause so great a scandal to all present, nor deceive the expectation of so many people. All those eyes, all those wills seem to weigh down upon you like a cope of lead, and, moreover, measures have been so well taken, everything has been so thoroughly arranged beforehand and after a fashion so evidently irrevocable, that the will yields to the weight of circumstances and utterly breaks down.

As the ceremony proceeded the features of the fair unknown changed their expression. Her look had at first been one of caressing tenderness; it changed to an air of disdain and of mortification, as though at not having been able to make itself understood.

With an effort of will sufficient to have uprooted a mountain, I strove to cry out that I would not be a priest, but I could not speak; my tongue seemed nailed to my palate, and I found it impossible to express my will by the least syllable of negation. Though fully awake, I felt like one under the influence of a nightmare, who vainly strives to shriek out the one word upon which life depends.

She seemed conscious of the martyrdom I was undergoing, and, as though to encourage me, she gave me a look replete with divinest promise. Her eyes were a poem; their every glance was a song.

She said to me:

'If thou wilt be mine, I shall make thee happier than God Himself in His paradise. The angels themselves will be jealous of thee. Tear off that funeral shroud in which thou art about to wrap thyself. I am Beauty, I am Youth, I am Life. Come to me! Together we shall be Love. Can Jehovah offer thee aught in exchange? Our lives will flow on like a dream, in one eternal kiss.

'Fling forth the wine of that chalice, and thou art free. I will conduct thee to the Unknown Isles. Thou shalt sleep in my bosom upon a bed of massy gold under a silver pavilion, for I love thee and would take thee away from thy God, before whom so many noble hearts pour forth floods of love which never reach even the steps of His throne!'

These words seemed to float to my ears in a rhythm of infinite sweetness, for her look was actually sonorous, and the utterances of her eyes were reechoed in the depths of my heart as though living lips had breathed them into my life. I felt myself willing to renounce God, and yet my tongue mechanically fulfilled all the formalities of the ceremony. The fair one gave me another look, so beseeching, so despairing that keen blades seemed to pierce my heart, and I felt my bosom transfixed by more swords than those of Our Lady of Sorrows.

All was consummated; I had become a priest.

Never was deeper anguish painted on human face than upon hers. The maiden who beholds her affianced lover suddenly fall dead at her side, the mother bending over the empty cradle of her child, Eve seated at the threshold of the gate of Paradise, the miser who finds a stone substituted for his stolen treasure, the poet who accidentally permits the only manuscript of his finest work to fall into the fire, could not wear a look so despairing, so inconsolable. All the blood had abandoned her charming face, leaving it whiter than marble; her beautiful arms hung lifelessly on either side of her body as though their muscles had suddenly relaxed, and she sought the support of a pillar, for her yielding limbs almost betrayed her. As for myself, I staggered toward the door of the church, livid as death, my forehead bathed with a sweat bloodier than that of Calvary; I felt as though I were being strangled; the vault seemed to have flattened down upon my shoulders, and it seemed to me that my head alone sustained the whole weight of the dome.

As I was about to cross the threshold a hand suddenly caught mine—a woman's hand! I had never till then touched the hand of any woman. It was cold as a serpent's skin, and yet its impress remained upon my wrist, burnt there as though branded by a glowing iron. It was she. 'Unhappy man! Unhappy man! What hast thou done?' she exclaimed in a low voice, and immediately disappeared in the crowd.

The aged bishop passed by. He cast a severe and scrutinising look upon me. My face presented the wildest aspect imaginable: I blushed and turned pale alternately; dazzling lights flashed before my eyes. A companion took pity on me. He seized my arm and led me out. I could not possibly have found my way back to the seminary unassisted. At the corner of a street, while the young priest's attention was momentarily turned in another direction, a negro page, fantastically garbed, approached me, and without pausing on his way slipped into my hand a little pocket-book with gold-embroidered corners, at the same time giving me a sign to hide it. I concealed it in my sleeve, and there kept it until I found myself alone in my cell. Then I opened the clasp. There were only two leaves within, bearing the words, 'Clarimonde. At the Concini Palace.' So little acquainted was I at that time with the things of this world that I had never heard of Clarimonde, celebrated as she was, and I had no idea as to where the Concini Palace was situated. I hazarded a thousand conjectures, each more extravagant than the last; but, in truth, I cared little whether she were a great lady or a courtesan, so that I could but see her once more.

My love, although the growth of a single hour, had taken imperishable root. I did not even dream of attempting to tear it up, so fully was I convinced such a thing would be impossible. That woman had completely taken possession of me. One look from her had sufficed to change my very nature. She had breathed her will into my life, and I no longer lived in myself, but in her and for her. I gave myself up to a thousand extravagancies. I kissed the place upon my hand which she had touched, and I repeated her name over and over again for hours in succession. I only needed to close my eyes in order to see her distinctly as though she were actually present; and I reiterated to myself the words she had uttered in my ear at the church porch: 'Unhappy man! Unhappy man! What hast thou done?' I comprehended at last the full horror of my situation, and the funereal and awful restraints of the state into which I had just entered became clearly revealed to me. To be a priest!—that is, to be chaste, to never love, to observe no distinction of sex or age, to turn from the sight of all beauty, to put out one's own eyes, to hide for ever crouching in the chill shadows of some church or cloister, to visit none but the dying, to watch by unknown corpses, and ever bear about with one the black soutane as a garb of mourning for oneself, so that your very dress might serve as a pall for your coffin.

And I felt life rising within me like a subterranean lake, expanding and overflowing; my blood leaped fiercely through my arteries; my long-restrained youth suddenly burst into active being, like the aloe which blooms but once in a hundred years, and then bursts into blossom with a clap of thunder.

What could I do in order to see Clarimonde once more? I had no pretext to offer for desiring to leave the seminary, not knowing any person in the city. I would not even be able to remain there but a short time, and was only waiting my assignment to the curacy which I must thereafter occupy. I tried to remove the bars of the window; but it was at a fearful height from the ground, and I found that as I had no ladder it would be useless to think of escaping thus. And, furthermore, I could descend thence only by night in any event, and afterward how should I be able to find my way through the inextricable labyrinth of streets? All these difficulties, which to many would have appeared altogether insignificant, were gigantic to me, a poor seminarist who had fallen in love only the day before for the first time, without experience, without money, without attire.

'Ah!' cried I to myself in my blindness, 'were I not a priest I could have seen her every day; I might have been her lover, her spouse. Instead of being wrapped in this dismal shroud of mine I would have had garments of silk and velvet, golden chains, a sword, and fair plumes like other handsome young cavaliers. My hair, instead of being dishonoured by the tonsure, would flow down upon my neck in waving curls; I would have a fine waxed moustache; I would be a gallant.' But one hour passed before an altar, a few hastily articulated words, had for ever cut me off from the number of the living, and I had myself sealed down the stone of my own tomb; I had with my own hand bolted the gate of my prison! I went to the window. The sky was beautifully blue; the trees had donned their spring robes; nature seemed to be making parade of an ironical joy. The *Place* was filled with people, some going, others coming; young beaux and young beauties were sauntering in couples toward the groves and gardens; merry youths passed by, cheerily trolling refrains of drinking-songs—it was all a picture of vivacity, life, animation, gaiety, which formed a bitter contrast with my mourning and my solitude. On the steps of the gate sat a young mother playing with her child. She kissed its little rosy mouth still impearled with drops of milk, and performed, in order to amuse it, a thousand divine little puerilities such as only mothers know how to invent. The father standing at a little distance smiled gently upon the charming group, and with folded arms seemed to hug his joy to his heart. I could not endure that spectacle. I closed the window with violence, and flung myself on my bed, my heart filled with frightful hate and jealousy, and gnawed my fingers and my bedcovers like a tiger that has passed ten days without food.

I know not how long I remained in this condition, but at last, while writhing on the bed in a fit of spasmodic fury, I suddenly perceived the Abbé Sérapion, who was standing erect in the centre of the room, watching me attentively. Filled with shame of myself, I let my head fall upon my breast and covered my face with my hands.

'Romuald, my friend, something very extraordinary is transpiring within you,' observed Sérapion, after a few moments' silence; 'your conduct is altogether inexplicable. You—always so quiet, so pious, so gentle—you to rage in your cell like a wild beast! Take heed, brother—do not listen to the suggestions of the devil The Evil Spirit, furious that you have consecrated yourself for ever to the Lord, is prowling around you like a ravening wolf and making a last effort to obtain possession of you. Instead of allowing yourself to be conquered, my dear Romuald, make to yourself a cuirass of prayers, a buckler of mortifications, and combat the enemy like a valiant man; you will then assuredly overcome him. Virtue must be proved by temptation, and gold comes forth purer from the hands of the assayer. Fear not. Never allow yourself to become discouraged. The most watchful and steadfast souls are at moments liable to such temptation. Pray, fast, meditate, and the Evil Spirit will depart from you.'

The words of the Abbé Sérapion restored me to myself, and I became a little more calm. 'I came,' he continued, 'to tell you that you have been appointed to the curacy of C—. The priest who had charge of it has just died, and Monseigneur the Bishop has ordered me to have you installed there at once. Be ready, therefore, to start tomorrow.' I responded with an inclination of the head, and the Abbé retired. I opened my missal and commenced reading some prayers, but the letters became confused and blurred under my eyes, the thread of the ideas entangled itself hopelessly in my brain, and the volume at last fell from my hands without my being aware of it.

To leave tomorrow without having been able to see her again, to add yet another barrier to the many already interposed between us, to lose for ever all hope of being able to meet her, except, indeed, through a miracle! Even to write to her, alas! would be impossible, for by whom could I dispatch my letter? With my sacred character of priest, to whom could I dare unbosom myself, in whom could I confide? I became a prey to the bitterest anxiety.

Then suddenly recurred to me the words of the Abbé Sérapion regarding the artifices of the devil; and the strange character of the adventure, the supernatural beauty of Clarimonde, the phosphoric light of her eyes, the burning imprint of her hand, the agony into which she had thrown me, the sudden change wrought within me when all my piety vanished in a single instant—these and other things clearly testified to the work of the Evil One, and perhaps that satiny hand was but the glove which concealed his claws. Filled with terror at these fancies, I again picked up the missal which had slipped from my knees and fallen upon the floor, and once more gave myself up to prayer.

Next morning Sérapion came to take me away. Two mules freighted with our miserable valises awaited us at the gate. He mounted one, and I the other as well as I knew how.

As we passed along the streets of the city, I gazed attentively at all the windows and balconies in the hope of seeing Clarimonde, but it was yet early in the morning, and the city had hardly opened its eyes. Mine sought to penetrate the blinds and window-curtains of all the palaces before which we were passing. Sérapion doubtless attributed this curiosity to my admiration of the architecture, for he slackened the pace of his animal in order to give me time to look around me. At last we passed the city gates and commenced to mount the hill beyond. When we arrived at its summit I turned to take a last look at the place where Clarimonde dwelt. The shadow of a great cloud hung over all the city; the contrasting colours of its blue and red roofs were lost in the uniform half-tint, through which here and there floated upward, like white flakes of foam, the smoke of freshly kindled fires. By a singular optical effect one edifice, which surpassed in height all the neighbouring buildings that were still dimly veiled by the vapours, towered up, fair and lustrous with the gilding of a solitary beam of sunlight—although actually more than a league away it seemed quite near. The smallest details of its architecture were plainly distinguishable—the turrets, the platforms, the window-casements, and even the swallow-tailed weather-vanes.

'What is that palace I see over there, all lighted up by the sun?' I asked Sérapion. He shaded his eyes with his hand, and having looked in the direction indicated, replied: 'It is the ancient palace which the Prince Concini has given to the courtesan Clarimonde. Awful things are done there!'

At that instant, I know not yet whether it was a reality or an illusion, I fancied I saw gliding along the terrace a shapely white figure, which gleamed for a moment in passing and as quickly vanished. It was Clarimonde.

Oh, did she know that at that very hour, all feverish and restless—from the height of the rugged road which separated me from her, and which, alas! I could never more descend—I was directing my eyes upon the palace where she dwelt, and which a mocking beam of sunlight seemed to bring nigh to me, as though inviting me to enter therein as its lord? Undoubtedly she must have known it, for her soul was too sympathetically united with mine not to have felt its least emotional thrill, and that subtle sympathy it must have been which prompted her to climb—although clad only in her nightdress—to the summit of the terrace, amid the icy dews of the morning.

The shadow gained the palace, and the scene became to the eye only a motionless ocean of roofs and gables, amid which one mountainous undulation was distinctly visible. Sérapion urged his mule forward, my own at once followed at the same gait, and a sharp angle in the road at last hid the city of S—for ever from my eyes, as I was destined never to return thither. At the close of a weary three-days' journey through dismal country fields, we caught sight of the cock upon the steeple of the church which I was to take charge of, peeping above the trees, and after having followed some winding roads fringed with thatched cottages and little gardens, we found ourselves in front of the façade, which certainly possessed few features of magnificence. A porch ornamented with some mouldings, and two or three pillars rudely hewn from sandstone; a tiled roof with counterforts of the same sandstone as the pillars—that was all. To the left lay the cemetery, overgrown with high weeds, and having a great iron cross rising up in its centre;

to the right stood the presbytery under the shadow of the church. It was a house of the most extreme simplicity and frigid cleanliness. We entered the enclosure. A few chickens were picking up some oats scattered upon the ground; accustomed, seemingly, to the black habit of ecclesiastics, they showed no fear of our presence and scarcely troubled themselves to get out of our way. A hoarse, wheezy barking fell upon our ears, and we saw an aged dog running toward us.

It was my predecessor's dog. He had dull bleared eyes, grizzled hair, and every mark of the greatest age to which a dog can possibly attain. I patted him gently, and he proceeded at once to march along beside me with an air of satisfaction unspeakable. A very old woman, who had been the housekeeper of the former curé, also came to meet us, and after having invited me into a little back parlour, asked whether I intended to retain her. I replied that I would take care of her, and the dog, and the chickens, and all the furniture her master had bequeathed her at his death. At this she became fairly transported with joy, and the Abbé Sérapion at once paid her the price which she asked for her little property.

As soon as my installation was over, the Abbé Sérapion returned to the seminary. I was, therefore, left alone, with no one but myself to look to for aid or counsel. The thought of Clarimonde again began to haunt me, and in spite of all my endeavours to banish it, I always found it present in my meditations. One evening, while promenading in my little garden along the walks bordered with box-plants, I fancied that I saw through the elm-trees the figure of a woman, who followed my every movement, and that I beheld two sea-green eyes gleaming through the foliage; but it was only an illusion, and on going round to the other side of the garden, I could find nothing except a footprint on the sanded walk—a footprint so small that it seemed to have been made by the foot of a child. The garden was enclosed by very high walls. I searched every nook and corner of it, but could discover no one there. I have never succeeded in fully accounting for this circumstance, which, after all, was nothing compared with the strange things which happened to me afterward.

For a whole year I lived thus, filling all the duties of my calling with the most scrupulous exactitude, praying and fasting, exhorting and lending ghostly aid to the sick, and bestowing alms even to the extent of frequently depriving myself of the very necessaries of life. But I felt a great aridness within me, and the sources of grace seemed closed against me. I never found that happiness which should spring from the fulfilment of a holy mission; my thoughts were far away, and the words of Clarimonde were ever upon my lips like an involuntary refrain. Oh, brother, meditate well on this! Through having but once lifted my eyes to look upon a woman, through one fault apparently so venial, I have for years remained a victim to the most miserable agonies, and the happiness of my life has been destroyed for ever.

I will not longer dwell upon those defeats, or on those inward victories invariably followed by yet more terrible falls, but will at once proceed to the facts of my story. One night my door-bell was long and violently rung. The aged housekeeper arose and opened to the stranger, and the figure of a man, whose complexion was deeply bronzed, and who was richly clad in a foreign costume, with a poniard at his girdle, appeared under the rays of Barbara's lantern. Her first impulse was one of terror, but the stranger reassured her, and stated that he desired to see me at once on matters relating to my holy calling. Barbara invited him upstairs, where I was on the point of retiring. The stranger told me that his mistress, a very noble lady, was lying at the point of death, and desired to see a priest. I replied that I was prepared to follow him, took with me the sacred articles necessary for extreme unction, and descended in all haste. Two horses black as the night itself stood without the gate, pawing the ground with impatience, and veiling their chests with long streams of smoky vapour exhaled from their nostrils. He held the stirrup and aided me to mount upon one; then, merely laying his hand upon the pommel of the saddle, he vaulted on the other, pressed the animal's sides with his knees, and loosened rein. The horse bounded forward with the velocity of an arrow. Mine, of which the stranger held the bridle, also started off at a swift gallop, keeping up with his companion. We devoured the road. The ground flowed backward beneath us in a long streaked line of pale gray, and the black silhouettes of the trees seemed fleeing by us on either side like an army in rout. We passed through a forest so profoundly gloomy that I felt my flesh creep in the chill darkness with superstitious fear. The showers of bright sparks which flew from the stony road under the ironshod feet of our horses remained glowing in our wake like a fiery trail; and had any one at that hour of the night beheld us both—my guide and myself—he must have taken us for two spectres riding upon nightmares. Witch-fires ever and anon flitted across the road before us, and the night-birds shrieked fearsomely in the depth of the woods beyond, where we beheld at intervals glow the phosphorescent eyes of wild cats. The manes of the horses became more and more dishevelled, the sweat streamed over their flanks, and their breath came through their nostrils hard and fast. But when he found them slacking pace, the guide reanimated them by uttering a strange, gutteral, unearthly cry, and the gallop recommenced with fury. At last the whirlwind race ceased; a huge black mass pierced through with many bright points of light suddenly rose before us, the hoofs of our horses echoed louder upon a strong wooden drawbridge, and we rode under a great vaulted archway which darkly yawned between two enormous towers. Some great excitement evidently reigned in the castle. Servants with torches were crossing the courtyard in every direction, and above lights were ascending and descending from landing to landing. I obtained a confused glimpse of vast masses of architecture—columns, arcades, flights of steps, stairways—a royal voluptuousness and elfin magnificence of construction worthy of fairyland. A negro page—the same who had before brought me the tablet from Clarimonde, and whom I instantly recognised—approached to aid me in dismounting, and the major-domo, attired in black velvet with a gold chain about his neck, advanced to meet me, supporting himself upon an ivory cane. Large tears were falling from his eyes and streaming over his cheeks and white beard. 'Too late!' he cried, sorrowfully shaking his venerable head. 'Too late, sir priest! But if you have not been able to save the soul, come at least to watch by the poor body.'

He took my arm and conducted me to the death-chamber. I wept not less bitterly than he, for I had learned that the dead one was none other than that Clarimonde whom I had so deeply and so wildly loved. A *prie-dieu* stood at the foot of the bed; a bluish flame flickering in a bronze patern filled all the room with a wan, deceptive light, here and there bringing out in the darkness at intervals some projection of furniture or cornice. In a chiselled urn upon the table there was a faded white rose, whose leaves—excepting one that still held—had all fallen, like odorous tears, to the foot of the vase. A broken black mask, a fan, and disguises of every variety, which were lying on the armchairs, bore witness that death had entered suddenly and unannounced into that sumptuous dwelling. Without daring to cast my eyes upon the bed, I knelt down and commenced to repeat the Psalms for the Dead, with exceeding fervour, thanking God that He had placed the tomb between me and the memory of this woman, so that I might thereafter be able to utter her name in my prayers as a name for ever sanctified by death. But my fervour gradually weakened, and I fell insensibly into a reverie. That chamber bore no semblance to a chamber of death. In lieu of the fetid and cadaverous odours which I had been accustomed to breathe during such funereal vigils, a languorous vapour of Oriental perfume—I know not what amorous odour of woman—softly floated through the tepid air. That pale light seemed rather a twilight gloom contrived for voluptuous pleasure, than a substitute for the yellow-flickering watch-tapers which shine by the side of corpses. I thought upon the strange destiny which enabled me to meet Clarimonde again at the very moment when she was lost to me for ever, and a sigh of regretful anguish escaped from my breast. Then it seemed to me that some one behind me had also sighed, and I turned round to look. It was only an echo. But in that moment my eyes fell upon the bed of death which they had till then avoided. The red damask curtains, decorated with large flowers worked in embroidery and looped up with gold bullion, permitted me to behold the fair dead, lying at full length, with hands joined upon her bosom. She was covered with a linen wrapping of dazzling whiteness, which formed a strong contrast with the gloomy purple of the hangings, and was of so fine a texture that it concealed nothing of her body's charming form, and allowed the eye to follow those beautiful outlines—undulating like the neck of a swan—which even death had not robbed of their supple grace. She seemed an alabaster statue executed by some skilful sculptor to place upon the tomb of a queen, or rather, perhaps, like a slumbering maiden over whom the silent snow had woven a spotless veil.

    I could no longer maintain my constrained attitude of prayer. The air of the alcove intoxicated me, that febrile perfume of half-faded roses penetrated my very brain, and I commenced to pace restlessly up and down the chamber, pausing at each turn before the bier to contemplate the graceful corpse lying beneath the transparency of its shroud. Wild fancies came thronging to my brain. I thought to myself that she might not, perhaps, be really dead; that she might only have feigned death for the purpose of bringing me to her castle, and then declaring her love. At one time I even thought I saw her foot move under the whiteness of the coverings, and slightly disarrange the long straight folds of the winding-sheet.

And then I asked myself: 'Is this indeed Clarimonde? What proof have I that it is she? Might not that black page have passed into the service of some other lady? Surely, I must be going mad to torture and afflict myself thus!' But my heart answered with a fierce throbbing: 'It is she; it is she indeed!' I approached the bed again, and fixed my eyes with redoubled attention upon the object of my incertitude. Ah, must I confess it? That exquisite perfection of bodily form, although purified and made sacred by the shadow of death, affected me more voluptuously than it should have done; and that repose so closely resembled slumber that one might well have mistaken it for such. I forgot that I had come there to perform a funeral ceremony; I fancied myself a young bridegroom entering the chamber of the bride, who all modestly hides her fair face, and through coyness seeks to keep herself wholly veiled. Heartbroken with grief, yet wild with hope, shuddering at once with fear and pleasure, I bent over her and grasped the corner of the sheet. I lifted it back, holding my breath all the while through fear of waking her. My arteries throbbed with such violence that I felt them hiss through my temples, and the sweat poured from my forehead in streams, as though I had lifted a mighty slab of marble. There, indeed, lay Clarimonde, even as I had seen her at the church on the day of my ordination. She was not less charming than then. With her, death seemed but a last coquetry. The pallor of her cheeks, the less brilliant carnation of her lips, her long eyelashes lowered and relieving their dark fringe against that white skin, lent her an unspeakably seductive aspect of melancholy chastity and mental suffering; her long loose hair, still intertwined with some little blue flowers, made a shining pillow for her head, and veiled the nudity of her shoulders with its thick ringlets; her beautiful hands, purer, more diaphanous, than the Host, were crossed on her bosom in an attitude of pious rest and silent prayer, which served to counteract all that might have proven otherwise too alluring—even after death—in the exquisite roundness and ivory polish of her bare arms from which the pearl bracelets had not yet been removed. I remained long in mute contemplation, and the more I gazed, the less could I persuade myself that life had really abandoned that beautiful body for ever. I do not know whether it was an illusion or a reflection of the lamplight, but it seemed to me that the blood was again commencing to circulate under that lifeless pallor, although she remained all motionless. I laid my hand lightly on her arm; it was cold, but not colder than her hand on the day when it touched mine at the portals of the church. I resumed my position, bending my face above her, and bathing her cheek with the warm dew of my tears. Ah, what bitter feelings of despair and helplessness, what agonies unutterable did I endure in that long watch! Vainly did I wish that I could have gathered all my life into one mass that I might give it all to her, and breathe into her chill remains the flame which devoured me. The night advanced, and feeling the moment of eternal separation approach, I could not deny myself the last sad sweet pleasure of imprinting a kiss upon the dead lips of her who had been my only love . . . Oh, miracle! A faint breath mingled itself with my breath, and the mouth of Clarimonde responded to the passionate pressure of mine. Her eyes unclosed, and lighted up with something of their former brilliancy; she uttered a long sigh, and uncrossing her arms, passed them around my neck with a look of ineffable delight. 'Ah, it is thou, Romuald!' she murmured in a voice languishingly sweet as the last vibrations of a harp. 'What ailed thee, dearest? I waited so long for thee that I am dead; but we are now betrothed: I can see thee and visit thee. Adieu, Romuald, adieu! I love thee. That is all I wished to tell thee, and I give thee back the life which thy kiss for a moment recalled. We shall soon meet again.'

Her head fell back, but her arms yet encircled me, as though to retain me still. A furious whirlwind suddenly burst in the window, and entered the chamber. The last remaining leaf of the white rose for a moment palpitated at the extremity of the stalk like a butterfly's wing, then it detached itself and flew forth through the open casement, bearing with it the soul of Clarimonde. The lamp was extinguished, and I fell insensible upon the bosom of the beautiful dead.

When I came to myself again I was lying on the bed in my little room at the presbytery, and the old dog of the former curé was licking my hand, which had been hanging down outside of the covers. Barbara, all trembling with age and anxiety, was busying herself about the room, opening and shutting drawers, and emptying powders into glasses. On seeing me open my eyes, the old woman uttered a cry of joy, the dog yelped and wagged his tail, but I was still so weak that I could not speak a single word or make the slightest motion. Afterward I learned that I had lain thus for three days, giving no evidence of life beyond the faintest respiration. Those three days do not reckon in my life, nor could I ever imagine whither my spirit had departed during those three days; I have no recollection of aught relating to them. Barbara told me that the same coppery-complexioned man who came to seek me on the night of my departure from the presbytery had brought me back the next morning in a close litter, and departed immediately afterward. When I became able to collect my scattered thoughts, I reviewed within my mind all the circumstances of that fateful night. At first I thought I had been the victim of some magical illusion, but ere long the recollection of other circumstances, real and palpable in themselves, came to forbid that supposition. I could not believe that I had been dreaming, since Barbara as well as myself had seen the strange man with his two black horses, and described with exactness every detail of his figure and apparel. Nevertheless it appeared that none knew of any castle in the neighbourhood answering to the description of that in which I had again found Clarimonde.

One morning I found the Abbé Sérapion in my room. Barbara had advised him that I was ill, and he had come with all speed to see me. Although this haste on his part testified to an affectionate interest in me, yet his visit did not cause me the pleasure which it should have done. The Abbé Sérapion had something penetrating and inquisitorial in his gaze which made me feel very ill at ease. His presence filled me with embarrassment and a sense of guilt. At the first glance he divined my interior trouble, and I hated him for his clairvoyance.

While he inquired after my health in hypocritically honeyed accents, he constantly kept his two great yellow lion-eyes fixed upon me, and plunged his look into my soul like a sounding-lead. Then he asked me how I directed my parish, if I was happy in it, how I passed the leisure hours allowed me in the intervals of pastoral duty, whether I had become acquainted with many of the inhabitants of the place, what was my favourite reading, and a thousand other such questions. I answered these inquiries as briefly as possible, and he, without ever waiting for my answers, passed rapidly from one subject of query to another. That conversation had evidently no connection with what he actually wished to say. At last, without any premonition, but as though repeating a piece of news which he had recalled on the instant, and feared might otherwise be forgotten subsequently, he suddenly said, in a clear vibrant voice, which rang in my ears like the trumpets of the Last Judgment:

'The great courtesan Clarimonde died a few days ago, at the close of an orgie which lasted eight days and eight nights. It was something infernally splendid. The abominations of the banquets of Belshazzar and Cleopatra were re-enacted there. Good God, what age are we living in? The guests were served by swarthy slaves who spoke an unknown tongue, and who seemed to me to be veritable demons. The livery of the very least among them would have served for the gala-dress of an emperor. There have always been very strange stories told of this Clarimonde, and all her lovers came to a violent or miserable end. They used to say that she was a ghoul, a female vampire; but I believe she was none other than Beelzebub himself.'

He ceased to speak, and commenced to regard me more attentively than ever, as though to observe the effect of his words on me. I could not refrain from starting when I heard him utter the name of Clarimonde, and this news of her death, in addition to the pain it caused me by reason of its coincidence with the nocturnal scenes I had witnessed, filled me with an agony and terror which my face betrayed, despite my utmost endeavours to appear composed. Sérapion fixed an anxious and severe look upon me, and then observed: 'My son, I must warn you that you are standing with foot raised upon the brink of an abyss; take heed lest you fall therein. Satan's claws are long, and tombs are not always true to their trust. The tombstone of Clarimonde should be sealed down with a triple seal, for, if report be true, it is not the first time she has died. May God watch over you, Romuald!'

And with these words the Abbé walked slowly to the door. I did not see him again at that time, for he left for S—almost immediately.

I became completely restored to health and resumed my accustomed duties. The memory of Clarimonde and the words of the old Abbé were constantly in my mind; nevertheless no extraordinary event had occurred to verify the funereal predictions of Sérapion, and I had commenced to believe that his fears and my own terrors were over-exaggerated, when one night I had a strange dream. I had hardly fallen asleep when I heard my bed-curtains drawn apart, as their rings slided back upon the curtain rod with a sharp sound. I rose up quickly upon my elbow, and beheld the shadow of a woman standing erect before me. I recognised Clarimonde immediately. She bore in her hand a little lamp, shaped like those which are placed in tombs, and its light lent her fingers a rosy transparency, which extended itself by lessening degrees even to the opaque and milky whiteness of her bare arm. Her only garment was the linen winding-sheet which had shrouded her when lying upon the bed of death. She sought to gather its folds over her bosom as though ashamed of being so scantily clad, but her little hand was not equal to the task. She was so white that the colour of the drapery blended with that of her flesh under the pallid rays of the lamp. Enveloped with this subtle tissue which betrayed all the contour of her body, she seemed rather the marble statue of some fair antique bather than a woman endowed with life. But dead or living, statue or woman, shadow or body, her beauty was still the same, only that the green light of her eyes was less brilliant, and her mouth, once so warmly crimson, was only tinted with a faint tender rosiness, like that of her cheeks. The little blue flowers which I had noticed entwined in her hair were withered and dry, and had lost nearly all their leaves, but this did not prevent her from being charming—so charming that, notwithstanding the strange character of the adventure, and the unexplainable manner in which she had entered my room, I felt not even for a moment the least fear.

She placed the lamp on the table and seated herself at the foot of my bed; then bending toward me, she said, in that voice at once silvery clear and yet velvety in its sweet softness, such as I never heard from any lips save hers:

'I have kept thee long in waiting, dear Romuald, and it must have seemed to thee that I had forgotten thee. But I come from afar off, very far off, and from a land whence no other has ever yet returned. There is neither sun nor moon in that land whence I come: all is but space and shadow; there is neither road nor pathway: no earth for the foot, no air for the wing; and nevertheless behold me here, for Love is stronger than Death and must conquer him in the end. Oh what sad faces and fearful things I have seen on my way hither! What difficulty my soul, returned to earth through the power of will alone, has had in finding its body and reinstating itself therein! What terrible efforts I had to make ere I could lift the ponderous slab with which they had covered me! See, the palms of my poor hands are all bruised! Kiss them, sweet love, that they may be healed!' She laid the cold palms of her hands upon ray mouth, one after the other. I kissed them, indeed, many times, and she the while watched me with a smile of ineffable affection.

I confess to my shame that I had entirely forgotten the advice of the Abbé Sérapion and the sacred office wherewith I had been invested. I had fallen without resistance, and at the first assault. I had not even made the least effort to repel the tempter. The fresh coolness of Clarimonde's skin penetrated my own, and I felt voluptuous tremors pass over my whole body. Poor child! in spite of all I saw afterward, I can hardly yet believe she was a demon; at least she had no appearance of being such, and never did Satan so skilfully conceal his claws and horns. She had drawn her feet up beneath her, and squatted down on the edge of the couch in an attitude full of negligent coquetry. From time to time she passed her little hand through my hair and twisted it into curls, as though trying how a new style of wearing it would become my face. I abandoned myself to her hands with the most guilty pleasure, while she accompanied her gentle play with the prettiest prattle. The most remarkable fact was that I felt no astonishment whatever at so extraordinary ah adventure, and as in dreams one finds no difficulty in accepting the most fantastic events as simple facts, so all these circumstances seemed to me perfectly natural in themselves.

'I loved thee long ere I saw thee, dear Romuald, and sought thee everywhere. Thou wast my dream, and I first saw thee in the church at the fatal moment. I said at once, "It is he!" I gave thee a look into which I threw all the love I ever had, all the love I now have, all the love I shall ever have for thee—a look that would have damned a cardinal or brought a king to his knees at my feet in view of all his court. Thou remainedst unmoved, preferring thy God to me!

'Ah, how jealous I am of that God whom thou didst love and still lovest more than me!

'Woe is me, unhappy one that I am! I can never have thy heart all to myself, I whom thou didst recall to life with a kiss—dead Clarimonde, who for thy sake bursts asunder the gates of the tomb, and comes to consecrate to thee a life which she has resumed only to make thee happy!'

All her words were accompanied with the most impassioned caresses, which bewildered my sense and my reason to such an extent, that I did not fear to utter a frightful blasphemy for the sake of consoling her, and to declare that I loved her as much as God.

Her eyes rekindled and shone like chrysoprases. 'In truth?—in very truth?—as much as God!' she cried, flinging her beautiful arms around me. 'Since it is so, thou wilt come with me; thou wilt follow me whithersoever I desire. Thou wilt cast away thy ugly black habit. Thou shalt be the proudest and most envied of cavaliers; thou shalt be my lover! To be the acknowledged lover of Clarimonde, who has refused even a Pope! That will be something to feel proud of. Ah, the fair, unspeakably happy existence, the beautiful golden life we shall live together! And when shall we depart, my fair sir?'

'Tomorrow! Tomorrow!' I cried in my delirium.

'Tomorrow, then, so let it be!' she answered. 'In the meanwhile I shall have opportunity to change my toilet, for this is a little too light and in nowise suited for a voyage. I must also forthwith notify all my friends who believe me dead, and mourn for me as deeply as they are capable of doing. The money, the dresses, the carriages—all will be ready. I shall call for thee at this same hour. Adieu, dear heart!' And she lightly touched my forehead with her lips. The lamp went out, the curtains closed again, and all became dark; a leaden, dreamless sleep fell on me and held me unconscious until the morning following.

I awoke later than usual, and the recollection of this singular adventure troubled me during the whole day. I finally persuaded myself that it was a mere vapour of my heated imagination. Nevertheless its sensations had been so vivid that it was difficult to persuade myself that they were not real, and it was not without some presentiment of what was going to happen that I got into bed at last, after having prayed God to drive far from me all thoughts of evil, and to protect the chastity of my slumber.

I soon fell into a deep sleep, and my dream was continued. The curtains again parted, and I beheld Clarimonde, not as on the former occasion, pale in her pale winding-sheet, with the violets of death upon her cheeks, but gay, sprightly, jaunty, in a superb travelling-dress of green velvet, trimmed with gold lace, and looped up on either side to allow a glimpse of satin petticoat. Her blond hair escaped in thick ringlets from beneath a broad black felt hat, decorated with white feathers whimsically twisted into various shapes. In one hand she held a little riding-whip terminated by a golden whistle. She tapped me lightly with it, and exclaimed: 'Well, my fine sleeper, is this the way you make your preparations? I thought I would find you up and dressed. Arise quickly, we have no time to lose.'

I leaped out of bed at once.

'Come, dress yourself, and let us go,' she continued, pointing to a little package she had brought with her. 'The horses are becoming impatient of delay and champing their bits at the door. We ought to have been by this time at least ten leagues distant from here.'

I dressed myself hurriedly, and she handed me the articles of apparel herself one by one, bursting into laughter from time to time at my awkwardness, as she explained to me the use of a garment when I had made a mistake. She hurriedly arranged my hair, and this done, held up before me a little pocket-mirror of Venetian crystal, rimmed with silver filigree-work, and playfully asked: 'How dost find thyself now? Wilt engage me for thy valet de chambre?'

I was no longer the same person, and I could not even recognise myself. I resembled my former self no more than a finished statue resembles a block of stone. My old face seemed but a coarse daub of the one reflected in the mirror. I was handsome, and my vanity was sensibly tickled by the metamorphosis.

That elegant apparel, that richly embroidered vest had made of me a totally different personage, and I marvelled at the power of transformation owned by a few yards of cloth cut after a certain pattern. The spirit of my costume penetrated my very skin and within ten minutes more I had become something of a coxcomb.

In order to feel more at ease in my new attire, I took several turns up and down the room. Clari-monde watched me with an air of maternal pleasure, and appeared well satisfied with her work. 'Come, enough of this child's play! Let us start, Romuald, dear. We have far to go, and we may not get there in time.' She took my hand and led me forth. All the doors opened before her at a touch, and we passed by the dog without awaking him.

At the gate we found Margheritone waiting, the same swarthy groom who had once before been my-escort. He held the bridles of three horses, all black like those which bore us to the castle—one for me, one for him, one for Clarimonde. Those horses must have been Spanish genets born of mares fecundated by a zephyr, for they were fleet as the wind itself, and the moon, which had just risen at our departure to light us on the way, rolled over the sky like a wheel detached from her own chariot. We beheld her on the right leaping from tree to tree, and putting herself out of breath in the effort to keep up with us. Soon we came upon a level plain where, hard by a clump of trees, a carriage with four vigorous horses awaited us. We entered it, and the postillions urged their animals into a mad gallop. I had one arm around Clarimonde's waist, and one of her hands clasped in mine; her head leaned upon my shoulder, and I felt her bosom, half bare, lightly pressing against my arm. I had never known such intense happiness. In that hour I had forgotten everything, and I no more remembered having ever been a priest than I remembered what I had been doing in my mother's womb, so great was the fascination which the evil spirit exerted upon me. From that night my nature seemed in some sort to have become halved, and there were two men within me, neither of whom knew the other. At one moment I believed myself a priest who dreamed nightly that he was a gentleman, at another that I was a gentleman who dreamed he was a priest. I could no longer distinguish the dream from the reality, nor could I discover where the reality began or where ended the dream. The exquisite young lord and libertine railed at the priest, the priest loathed the dissolute habits of the young lord. Two spirals entangled and confounded the one with the other, yet never touching, would afford a fair representation of this bicephalic life which I lived. Despite the strange character of my condition, I do not believe that I ever inclined, even for a moment, to madness. I always retained with extreme vividness all the perceptions of my two lives. Only there was one absurd fact which I could not explain to myself—namely, that the consciousness of the same individuality existed in two men so opposite in character. It was an anomaly for which I could not account—whether I believed myself to be the curé of the little village of C—, or *Il Signor Romualdo*, the titled lover of Clarimonde.

Be that as it may, I lived, at least I believed that I lived, in Venice. I have never been able to discover rightly how much of illusion and how much of reality there was in this fantastic adventure. We dwelt in a great palace on the Canaleio, filled with frescoes and statues, and containing two Titians in the noblest style of the great master, which were hung in Clarimonde's chamber. It was a palace well worthy of a king. We had each our gondola, our *barcarolli* in family livery, our music hall, and our special poet. Clarimonde always lived upon a magnificent scale; there was something of Cleopatra in her nature. As for me, I had the retinue of a prince's son, and I was regarded with as much reverential respect as though I had been of the family of one of the twelve Apostles or the four Evangelists of the Most Serene Republic. I would not have turned aside to allow even the Doge to pass, and I do not believe that since Satan fell from heaven, any creature was ever prouder or more insolent than I. I went to the Ridotto, and played with a luck which seemed absolutely infernal. I received the best of all society—the sons of ruined families, women of the theatre, shrewd knaves, parasites, hectoring swashbucklers. But notwithstanding the dissipation of such a life, I always remained faithful to Clarimonde. I loved her wildly. She would have excited satiety itself, and chained inconstancy. To have Clarimonde was to have twenty mistresses; ay, to possess all women: so mobile, so varied of aspect, so fresh in new charms was she all in herself—a very chameleon of a woman, in sooth. She made you commit with her the infidelity you would have committed with another, by donning to perfection the character, the attraction, the style of beauty of the woman who appeared to please you. She returned my love a hundred-fold, and it was in vain that the young patricians and even the Ancients of the Council of Ten made her the most magnificent proposals. A Foscari even went so far as to offer to espouse her. She rejected all his overtures. Of gold she had enough. She wished no longer for anything but love—a love youthful, pure, evoked by herself, and which should be a first and last passion. I would have been perfectly happy but for a cursed nightmare which recurred every night, and in which I believed myself to be a poor village curé, practising mortification and penance for my excesses during the day. Reassured by my constant association with her, I never thought further of the strange manner in which I had become acquainted with Clarimonde. But the words of the Abbé Sérapion concerning her recurred often to my memory, and never ceased to cause me uneasiness.

For some time the health of Clarimonde had not been so good as usual; her complexion grew paler day by day. The physicians who were summoned could not comprehend the nature of her malady and knew not how to treat it. They all prescribed some insignificant remedies, and never called a second time. Her paleness, nevertheless, visibly increased, and she became colder and colder, until she seemed almost as white and dead as upon that memorable night in the unknown castle. I grieved with anguish unspeakable to behold her thus slowly perishing; and she, touched by my agony, smiled upon me sweetly and sadly with the fateful smile of those who feel that they must die.

One morning I was seated at her bedside, and breakfasting from a little table placed close at hand, so that I might not be obliged to leave her for a single instant. In the act of cutting some fruit I accidentally inflicted rather a deep gash on my finger. The blood immediately gushed forth in a little purple jet, and a few drops spurted upon Clarimonde. Her eyes flashed, her face suddenly assumed an expression of savage and ferocious joy such as I had never before observed in her. She leaped out of her bed with animal agility—the agility, as it were, of an ape or a cat—and sprang upon my wound, which she commenced to suck with an air of unutterable pleasure. She swallowed the blood in little mouthfuls, slowly and carefully, like a connoisseur tasting a wine from Xeres or Syracuse. Gradually her eyelids half closed, and the pupils of her green eyes became oblong instead of round. From time to time she paused in order to kiss my hand, then she would recommence to press her lips to the lips of the wound in order to coax forth a few more ruddy drops. When she found that the blood would no longer come, she arose with eyes liquid and brilliant, rosier than a May dawn; her face full and fresh, her hand warm and moist—in fine, more beautiful than ever, and in the most perfect health.

'I shall not die! I shall not die!' she cried, clinging to my neck, half mad with joy. 'I can love thee yet for a long time. My life is thine, and all that is of me comes from thee. A few drops of thy rich and noble blood, more precious and more potent than all the elixirs of the earth, have given me back life.'

This scene long haunted my memory, and inspired me with strange doubts in regard to Clarimonde; and the same evening, when slumber had transported me to my presbytery, I beheld the Abbé Sérapion, graver and more anxious of aspect than ever. He gazed attentively at me, and sorrowfully exclaimed: 'Not content with losing your soul, you now desire also to lose your body. Wretched young man, into how terrible a plight have you fallen!' The tone in which he uttered these words powerfully affected me, but in spite of its vividness even that impression was soon dissipated, and a thousand other cares erased it from my mind. At last one evening, while looking into a mirror whose traitorous position she had not taken into account, I saw Clarimonde in the act of emptying a powder into the cup of spiced wine which she had long been in the habit of preparing after our repasts. I took the cup, feigned to carry it to my lips, and then placed it on the nearest article of furniture as though intending to finish it at my leisure. Taking advantage of a moment when the fair one's back was turned, I threw the contents under the table, after which I retired to my chamber and went to bed, fully resolved not to sleep, but to watch and discover what should come of all this mystery. I did not have to wait long, Clarimonde entered in her nightdress, and having removed her apparel, crept into bed and lay down beside me. When she felt assured that I was asleep, she bared my arm, and drawing a gold pin from her hair, commenced to murmur in a low voice:

'One drop, only one drop! One ruby at the end of my needle . . . Since thou lovest me yet, I must not die! . . . Ah, poor love! His beautiful blood, so brightly purple, I must drink it. Sleep, my only treasure! Sleep, my god, my child! I will do thee no harm; I will only take of thy life what I must to keep my own from being for ever extinguished. But that I love thee so much, I could well resolve to have other lovers whose veins I could drain; but since I have known thee all other men have become hateful to me . . . Ah, the beautiful arm! How round it is! How white it is! How shall I ever dare to prick this pretty blue vein!' And while thus murmuring to herself she wept, and I felt her tears raining on my arm as she clasped it with her hands. At last she took the resolve, slightly punctured me with her pin, and commenced to suck up the blood which oozed from the place. Although she swallowed only a few drops, the fear of weakening me soon seized her, and she carefully tied a little band around my arm, afterward rubbing the wound with an unguent which immediately cicatrised it. Further doubts were impossible. The Abbé Sérapion was right. Notwithstanding this positive knowledge, however, I could not cease to love Clarimonde, and I would gladly of my own accord have given her all the blood she required to sustain her factitious life. Moreover, I felt but little fear of her. The woman seemed to plead with me for the vampire, and what I had already heard and seen sufficed to reassure me completely. In those days I had plenteous veins, which would not have been so easily exhausted as at present; and I would not have thought of bargaining for my blood, drop by drop. I would rather have opened myself the veins of my arm and said to her: 'Drink, and may my love infiltrate itself throughout thy body together with my blood!' I carefully avoided ever making the least reference to the narcotic drink she had prepared for me, or to the incident of the pin, and we lived in the most perfect harmony.

Yet my priestly scruples commenced to torment me more than ever, and I was at a loss to imagine what new penance I could invent in order to mortify and subdue my flesh. Although these visions were involuntary, and though I did not actually participate in anything relating to them, I could not dare to touch the body of Christ with hands so impure and a mind defiled by such debauches whether real or imaginary. In the effort to avoid falling under the influence of these wearisome hallucinations, I strove to prevent myself from being overcome by sleep. I held my eyelids open with my fingers, and stood for hours together leaning upright against the wall, fighting sleep with all my might; but the dust of drowsiness invariably gathered upon my eyes at last, and finding all resistance useless, I would have to let my arms fall in the extremity of despairing weariness, and the current of slumber would again bear me away to the perfidious shores. Sérapion addressed me with the most vehement exhortations, severely reproaching me for my softness and want of fervour. Finally, one day when I was more wretched than usual, he said to me: 'There is but one way by which you can obtain relief from this continual torment, and though it is an extreme measure it must be made use of; violent diseases require violent remedies. I know where Clarimonde is buried. It is necessary that we shall disinter her remains, and that you shall behold in how pitiable a state the object of your love is. Then you will no longer be tempted to lose your soul for the sake of an unclean corpse devoured by worms, and ready to crumble into dust. That will assuredly restore you to yourself.' For my part, I was so tired of this double life that I at once consented, desiring to ascertain beyond a doubt whether a priest or a gentleman had been the victim of delusion. I had become fully resolved either to kill one of the two men within me for the benefit of the other, or else to kill both, for so terrible an existence could not last long and be endured. The Abbé Sérapion provided himself with a mattock, a lever, and a lantern, and at midnight we wended our way to the cemetery of—, the location and place of which were perfectly familiar to him. After having directed the rays of the dark lantern upon the inscriptions of several tombs, we came at last upon a great slab, half concealed by huge weeds and devoured by mosses and parasitic plants, whereupon we deciphered the opening lines of the epitaph:

> Here lies Clarimonde
> Who was famed in her life-time
> As the fairest of women.*

> * Ici gît Clarimonde
> Qui fut de son vivant
> La plus belle du monde.

> The broken beauty of the lines is unavoidably
> lost in the translation.

'It is here without a doubt,' muttered Sérapion, and placing his lantern on the ground, he forced the point of the lever under the edge of the stone and commenced to raise it. The stone yielded, and he proceeded to work with the mattock. Darker and more silent than the night itself, I stood by and watched him do it, while he, bending over his dismal toil, streamed with sweat, panted, and his hard-coming breath seemed to have the harsh tone of a death rattle. It was a weird scene, and had any persons from without beheld us, they would assuredly have taken us rather for profane wretches and shroud-stealers than for priests of God. There was something grim and fierce in Sérapion's zeal which lent him the air of a demon rather than of an apostle or an angel, and his great aquiline face, with all its stern features, brought out in strong relief by the lantern-light, had something fearsome in it which enhanced the unpleasant fancy. I felt an icy sweat come out upon my forehead in huge beads, and my hair stood up with a hideous fear. Within the depths of my own heart I felt that the act of the austere Sérapion was an abominable sacrilege; and I could have prayed that a triangle of fire would issue from the entrails of the dark clouds, heavily rolling above us, to reduce him to cinders. The owls which had been nestling in the cypress-trees, startled by the gleam of the lantern, flew against it from time to time, striking their dusty wings against its panes, and uttering plaintive cries of lamentation; wild foxes yelped in the far darkness, and a thousand sinister noises detached themselves from the silence. At last Séra-pion's mattock struck the coffin itself, making its planks re-echo with a deep sonorous sound, with that terrible sound nothingness utters when stricken. He wrenched apart and tore up the lid, and I beheld Clarimonde, pallid as a figure of marble, with hands joined; her white winding-sheet made but one fold from her head to her feet. A little crimson drop sparkled like a speck of dew at one corner of her colourless mouth. Sérapion, at this spectacle, burst into fury: 'Ah, thou art here, demon! Impure courtesan! Drinker of blood and gold!' And he flung holy water upon the corpse and the coffin, over which he traced the sign of the cross with his sprinkler. Poor Clarimonde had no sooner been touched by the blessed spray than her beautiful body crumbled into dust, and became only a shapeless and frightful mass of cinders and half-calcined bones.

'Behold your mistress, my Lord Romuald!' cried the inexorable priest, as he pointed to these sad remains. 'Will you be easily tempted after this to promenade on the Lido or at Fusina with your beauty?' I covered my face with my hands, a vast ruin had taken place within me. I returned to my presbytery, and the noble Lord Romuald, the lover of Clarimonde, separated himself from the poor priest with whom he had kept such strange company so long. But once only, the following night, I saw Clarimonde. She said to me, as she had said the first time at the portals of the church: 'Unhappy man! Unhappy man! What hast thou done? Wherefore have hearkened to that imbecile priest? Wert thou not happy? And what harm had I ever done thee that thou shouldst violate my poor tomb, and lay bare the miseries of my nothingness? All communication between our souls and our bodies is henceforth for ever broken. Adieu! Thou wilt yet regret me!' She vanished in air as smoke, and I never saw her more.

Alas! she spoke truly indeed. I have regretted her more than once, and I regret her still. My soul's peace has been very dearly bought. The love of God was not too much to replace such a love as hers. And this, brother, is the story of my youth. Never gaze upon a woman, and walk abroad only with eyes ever fixed upon the ground; for however chaste and watchful one may be, the error of a single moment is enough to make one lose eternity. lose eternity.

THE MUMMY'S FOOT

I had entered, in an idle mood, the shop of one of those curiosity venders who are called *marchands de bric-à-brac* in that Parisian *argot* which is so perfectly unintelligible elsewhere in France.

You have doubtless glanced occasionally through the windows of some of these shops, which have become so numerous now that it is fashionable to buy antiquated furniture, and that every petty stockbroker thinks he must have his *chambre au moyen âge*.

There is one thing there which clings alike to the shop of the dealer in old iron, the ware-room of the tapestry maker, the laboratory of the chemist, and the studio of the painter: in all those gloomy dens where a furtive daylight filters in through the window-shutters the most manifestly ancient thing is dust. The cobwebs are more authentic than the gimp laces, and the old pear-tree furniture on exhibition is actually younger than the mahogany which arrived but yesterday from America.

The warehouse of my bric-à-brac dealer was a veritable Capharnaum. All ages and all nations seemed to have made their rendezvous there. An Etruscan lamp of red clay stood upon a Boule cabinet, with ebony panels, brightly striped by lines of inlaid brass; a duchess of the court of Louis xv. nonchalantly extended her fawn-like feet under a massive table of the time of Louis xiii., with heavy spiral supports of oak, and carven designs of chimeras and foliage intermingled.

Upon the denticulated shelves of several sideboards glittered immense Japanese dishes with red and blue designs relieved by gilded hatching, side by side with enamelled works by Bernard Palissy, representing serpents, frogs, and lizards in relief.

From disembowelled cabinets escaped cascades of silver-lustrous Chinese silks and waves of tinsel, which an oblique sunbeam shot through with luminous beads, while portraits of every era, in frames more or less tarnished, smiled through their yellow varnish.

The striped breastplate of a damascened suit of Milanese armour glittered in one corner; loves and nymphs of porcelain, Chinese grotesques, vases of *céladon* and crackleware, Saxon and old Sèvres cups encumbered the shelves and nooks of the apartment.

The dealer followed me closely through the tortuous way contrived between the piles of furniture, warding off with his hand the hazardous sweep of my coat-skirts, watching my elbows with the uneasy attention of an antiquarian and a usurer.

It was a singular face, that of the merchant; an immense skull, polished like a knee, and surrounded by a thin aureole of white hair, which brought out the clear salmon tint of his complexion all the more strikingly, lent him a false aspect of patriarchal *bonhomie*, counteracted, however, by the scintillation of two little yellow eyes which trembled in their orbits like two louis-d'or upon quicksilver. The curve of his nose presented an aquiline silhouette, which suggested the Oriental or Jewish type. His hands—thin, slender, full of nerves which projected like strings upon the finger-board of a violin, and armed with claws like those on the terminations of bats' wings—shook with senile trembling; but those convulsively agitated hands became firmer than steel pincers or lobsters' claws when they lifted any precious article—an onyx cup, a Venetian glass, or a dish of Bohemian crystal. This strange old man had an aspect so thoroughly rabbinical and cabalistic that he would have been burnt on the mere testimony of his face three centuries ago.

'Will you not buy something from me today, sir? Here is a Malay kreese with a blade undulating like flame. Look at those grooves contrived for the blood to run along, those teeth set backward so as to tear out the entrails in withdrawing the weapon. It is a fine character of ferocious arm, and will look well in your collection. This two-handed sword is very beautiful. It is the work of Josepe de la Hera; and this *colichemarde* with its fenestrated guard—what a superb specimen of handicraft!'

'No; I have quite enough weapons and instruments of carnage. I want a small figure,—something which will suit me as a paper-weight, for I cannot endure those trumpery bronzes which the stationers sell, and which may be found on everybody's desk.'

The old gnome foraged among his ancient wares, and finally arranged before me some antique bronzes, so-called at least; fragments of malachite, little Hindoo or Chinese idols, a kind of poussah-toys in jade-stone, representing the incarnations of Brahma or Vishnoo, and wonderfully appropriate to the very undivine office of holding papers and letters in place.

I was hesitating between a porcelain dragon, all constellated with warts, its mouth formidable with bristling tusks and ranges of teeth, and an abominable little Mexican fetich, representing the god Vitziliputzili *au naturel*, when I caught sight of a charming foot, which I at first took for a fragment of some antique Venus.

It had those beautiful ruddy and tawny tints that lend to Florentine bronze that warm living look so much preferable to the gray-green aspect of common bronzes, which might easily be mistaken for statues in a state of putrefaction. Satiny gleams played over its rounded forms, doubtless polished by the amorous kisses of twenty centuries, for it seemed a Corinthian bronze, a work of the best era of art, perhaps moulded by Lysippus himself.

'That foot will be my choice,' said to the merchant, who regarded me with an ironical and saturnine air, and held out the object desired that I might examine it more fully.

I was surprised at its lightness. It was not a foot of metal, but in sooth a foot of flesh, an embalmed foot, a mummy's foot. On examining it still more closely the very grain of the skin, and the almost imperceptible lines impressed upon it by the texture of the bandages, became perceptible. The toes were slender and delicate, and terminated by perfectly formed nails, pure and transparent as agates. The great toe, slightly separated from the rest, afforded a happy contrast, in the antique style, to the position of the other toes, and lent it an aerial lightness—the grace of a bird's foot. The sole, scarcely streaked by a few almost imperceptible cross lines, afforded evidence that it had never touched the bare ground, and had only come in contact with the finest matting of Nile rushes and the softest carpets of panther skin.

'Ha, ha, you want the foot of the Princess Hermonthis!' exclaimed the merchant, with a strange giggle, fixing his owlish eyes upon me. 'Ha, ha, ha! For a paper-weight! An original idea!—artistic idea!-Old Pharaoh would certainly have been surprised had some one told him that the foot of his adored daughter would be used for a paper-weight after he had had a mountain of granite hollowed out as a receptacle for the triple coffin, painted and gilded, covered with hieroglyphics and beautiful paintings of the Judgment of Souls,' continued the queer little merchant, half audibly, as though talking to himself.

'How much will you charge me for this mummy fragment?'

'Ah, the highest price I can get, for it is a superb piece. If I had the match of it you could not have it for less than five hundred francs. The daughter of a Pharaoh! Nothing is more rare.'

'Assuredly that is not a common article, but still, how much do you want? In the first place let me warn you that all my wealth consists of just five louis. I can buy anything that costs five louis, but nothing dearer. You might search my vest pockets and most secret drawers without even finding one poor five-franc piece more.'

'Five louis for the foot of the Princess Hermonthis! That is very little, very little indeed. 'Tis an authentic foot,' muttered the merchant, shaking his head, and imparting a peculiar rotary motion to his eyes. 'Well, take it, and I will give you the bandages into the bargain,' he added, wrapping the foot in an ancient damask rag. 'Very fine? Real damask—Indian damask which has never been redyed. It is strong, and yet it is soft,' he mumbled, stroking the frayed tissue with his fingers, through the trade-acquired habit which moved him to praise even an object of such little value that he himself deemed it only worth the giving away.

He poured the gold coins into a sort of mediaeval alms-purse hanging at his belt, repeating:

'The foot of the Princess Hermonthis to be used for a paper-weight!'

Then turning his phosphorescent eyes upon me, he exclaimed in a voice strident as the crying of a cat which has swallowed a fish-bone:

'Old Pharaoh will not be well pleased. He loved his daughter, the dear man!'

'You speak as if you were a contemporary of his. You are old enough, goodness knows! but you do not date back to the Pyramids of Egypt,' I answered, laughingly, from the threshold.

I went home, delighted with my acquisition.

With the idea of putting it to profitable use as soon as possible, I placed the foot of the divine Princess Hermonthis upon a heap of papers scribbled over with verses, in themselves an undecipherable mosaic work of erasures; articles freshly begun; letters forgotten, and posted in the table drawer instead of the letter-box, an error to which absent-minded people are peculiarly liable. The effect was charming, *bizarre*, and romantic.

Well satisfied with this embellishment, I went out with the gravity and pride becoming one who feels that he has the ineffable advantage over all the passers-by whom he elbows, of possessing a piece of the Princess Hermonthis, daughter of Pharaoh.

I looked upon all who did not possess, like myself, a paper-weight so authentically Egyptian as very ridiculous people, and it seemed to me that the proper occupation of every sensible man should consist in the mere fact of having a mummy's foot upon his desk.

Happily I met some friends, whose presence distracted me in my infatuation with this new acquisition. I went to dinner with them, for I could not very well have dined with myself.

When I came back that evening, with my brain slightly confused by a few glasses of wine, a vague whiff of Oriental perfume delicately titillated my olfactory nerves. The heat of the room had warmed the natron, bitumen, and myrrh in which the *paraschistes*, who cut open the bodies of the dead, had bathed the corpse of the princess. It was a perfume at once sweet and penetrating, a perfume that four thousand years had not been able to dissipate.

The Dream of Egypt was Eternity. Her odours have the solidity of granite and endure as long.

I soon drank deeply from the black cup of sleep. For a few hours all remained opaque to me. Oblivion and nothingness inundated me with their sombre waves.

Yet light gradually dawned upon the darkness of my mind. Dreams commenced to touch me softly in their silent flight.

The eyes of my soul were opened, and I beheld my chamber as it actually was. I might have believed myself awake but for a vague consciousness which assured me that I slept, and that something fantastic was about to take place.

The odour of the myrrh had augmented in intensity, and I felt a slight headache, which I very naturally attributed to several glasses of champagne that we had drunk to the unknown gods and our future fortunes.

I peered through my room with a feeling of expectation which I saw nothing to justify. Every article of furniture was in its proper place. The lamp, softly shaded by its globe of ground crystal, burned upon its bracket; the water-colour sketches shone under their Bohemian glass; the curtains hung down languidly; everything wore an aspect of tranquil slumber.

After a few moments, however, all this calm interior appeared to become disturbed. The woodwork cracked stealthily, the ash-covered log suddenly emitted a jet of blue flame, and the discs of the pateras seemed like great metallic eyes, watching, like myself, for the things which were about to happen.

My eyes accidentally fell upon the desk where I had placed the foot of the Princess Hermonthis.

Instead of remaining quiet, as behoved a foot which had been embalmed for four thousand years, it commenced to act in a nervous manner, contracted itself, and leaped over the papers like a startled frog. One would have imagined that it had suddenly been brought into contact with a galvanic battery. I could distinctly hear the dry sound made by its little heel, hard as the hoof of a gazelle.

I became rather discontented with my acquisition, inasmuch as I wished my paper-weights to be of a sedentary disposition, and thought it very unnatural that feet should walk about without legs, and I commenced to experience a feeling closely akin to fear.

Suddenly I saw the folds of my bed-curtain stir, and heard a bumping sound, like that caused by some person hopping on one foot across the floor. I must confess I became alternately hot and cold, that I felt a strange wind chill my back, and that my suddenly rising hair caused my night-cap to execute a leap of several yards.

The bed-curtains opened and I beheld the strangest figure imaginable before me.

It was a young girl of a very deep coffee-brown complexion, like the bayadère Amani, and possessing the purest Egyptian type of perfect beauty. Her eyes were almond shaped and oblique, with eyebrows so black that they seemed blue; her nose was exquisitely chiselled, almost Greek in its delicacy of outline; and she might indeed have been taken for a Corinthian statue of bronze but for the prominence of her cheek-bones and the slightly African fulness of her lips, which compelled one to recognise her as belonging beyond all doubt to the hieroglyphic race which dwelt upon the banks of the Nile.

Her arms, slender and spindle-shaped like those of very young girls, were encircled by a peculiar kind of metal bands and bracelets of glass beads; her hair was all twisted into little cords, and she wore upon her bosom a little idol-figure of green paste, bearing a whip with seven lashes, which proved it to be an image of Isis; her brow was adorned with a shining plate of gold, and a few traces of paint relieved the coppery tint of her cheeks.

As for her costume, it was very odd indeed.

Fancy a *pagne*, or skirt, all formed of little strips of material bedizened with red and black hieroglyphics, stiffened with bitumen, and apparently belonging to a freshly unbandaged mummy.

In one of those sudden flights of thought so common in dreams I heard the hoarse falsetto of the bric-à-brac dealer, repeating like a monotonous refrain the phrase he had uttered in his shop with so enigmatical an intonation:

'Old Pharaoh will not be well pleased He loved his daughter, the dear man!'

One strange circumstance, which was not at all calculated to restore my equanimity, was that the apparition had but one foot; the other was broken off at the ankle!

She approached the table where the foot was starting and fidgeting about more than ever, and there supported herself upon the edge of the desk. I saw her eyes fill with pearly gleaming tears.

Although she had not as yet spoken, I fully comprehended the thoughts which agitated her. She looked at her foot—for it was indeed her own—with an exquisitely graceful expression of coquettish sadness, but the foot leaped and ran hither and thither, as though impelled on steel springs.

Twice or thrice she extended her hand to seize it, but could not succeed.

Then commenced between the Princess Hermonthis and her foot—which appeared to be endowed with a special life of its own—a very fantastic dialogue in a most ancient Coptic tongue, such as might have been spoken thirty centuries ago in the syrinxes of the land of Ser. Luckily I understood Coptic perfectly well that night.

The Princess Hermonthis cried, in a voice sweet and vibrant as the tones of a crystal bell:

'Well, my dear little foot, you always flee from me, yet I always took good care of you. I bathed you with perfumed water in a bowl of alabaster; I smoothed your heel with pumice-stone mixed with palm-oil; your nails were cut with golden scissors and polished with a hippopotamus tooth; I was careful to select *tatbebs* for you, painted and embroidered and turned up at the toes, which were the envy of all the young girls in Egypt. You wore on your great toe rings bearing the device of the sacred Scarabseus, and you supported one of the lightest bodies that a lazy foot could sustain.'

The foot replied in a pouting and chagrined tone:

'You know well that I do not belong to myself any longer. I have been bought and paid for. The old merchant knew what he was about. He bore you a grudge for having refused to espouse him. This is an ill turn which he has done you. The Arab who violated your royal coffin in the subterranean pits of the necropolis of Thebes was sent thither by him. He desired to prevent you from being present at the reunion of the shadowy nations in the cities below. Have you five pieces of gold for my ransom?'

'Alas, no! My jewels, my rings, my purses of gold and silver were all stolen from me,' answered the Princess Hermonthis with a sob.

'Princess,' I then exclaimed, 'I never retained anybody's foot unjustly. Even though you have not got the five louis which it cost me, I present it to you gladly. I should feel unutterably wretched to think that I were the cause of so amiable a person as the Princess Hermonthis being lame.'

I delivered this discourse in a royally gallant, troubadour tone which must have astonished the beautiful Egyptian girl.

She turned a look of deepest gratitude upon me, and her eyes shone with bluish gleams of light.

She took her foot, which surrendered itself willingly this time, like a woman about to put on her little shoe, and adjusted it to her leg with much skill.

This operation over, she took a few steps about the room, as though to assure herself that she was really no longer lame.

'Ah, how pleased my father will be! He who was so unhappy because of my mutilation, and who from the moment of my birth set a whole nation at work to hollow me out a tomb so deep that he might preserve me intact until that last day when souls must be weighed in the balance of Amenthi! Come with me to my father. He will receive you kindly, for you have given me back my foot.'

I thought this proposition natural enough. I arrayed myself in a dressing-gown of large-flowered pattern, which lent me a very Pharaonic aspect, hurriedly put on a pair of Turkish slippers, and informed the Princess Hermonthis that I was ready to follow her.

Before starting, Hermonthis took from her neck the little idol of green paste, and laid it on the scattered sheets of paper which covered the table.

'It is only fair,' she observed, smilingly, 'that I should replace your paper-weight.'

She gave me her hand, which felt soft and cold, like the skin of a serpent, and we departed.

We passed for some time with the velocity of an arrow through a fluid and grayish expanse, in which half-formed silhouettes flitted swiftly by us, to right and left.

For an instant we saw only sky and sea.

A few moments later obelisks commenced to tower in the distance; pylons and vast flights of steps guarded by sphinxes became clearly outlined against the horizon.

We had reached our destination.

The princess conducted me to a mountain of rose-coloured granite, in the face of which appeared an opening so narrow and low that it would have been difficult to distinguish it from the fissures in the rock, had not its location been marked by two stelae wrought with sculptures.

Hermonthis kindled a torch and led the way before me.

We traversed corridors hewn through the living rock. Their walls, covered with hieroglyphics and paintings of allegorical processions, might well have occupied thousands of arms for thousands of years in their formation. These corridors of interminable length opened into square chambers, in the midst of which pits had been contrived, through which we descended by cramp-irons or spiral stairways. These pits again conducted us into other chambers, opening into other corridors, likewise decorated with painted sparrow-hawks, serpents coiled in circles, the symbols of the *tau* and *pedum*—prodigious works of art which no living eye can ever examine—interminable legends of granite which only the dead have time to read through all eternity.

At last we found ourselves in a hall so vast, so enormous, so immeasurable, that the eye could not reach its limits. Files of monstrous columns stretched far out of sight on every side, between which twinkled livid stars of yellowish flame; points of light which revealed further depths incalculable in the darkness beyond.

The Princess Hermonthis still held my hand, and graciously saluted the mummies of her acquaintance.

My eyes became accustomed to the dim twilight, and objects became discernible.

I beheld the kings of the subterranean races seated upon thrones—grand old men, though dry, withered, wrinkled like parchment, and blackened with naphtha and bitumen—all wearing *pshents* of gold, and breastplates and gorgets glittering with precious stones, their eyes immovably fixed like the eyes of sphinxes, and their long beards whitened by the snow of centuries. Behind them stood their peoples, in the stiff and constrained posture enjoined by Egyptian art, all eternally preserving the attitude prescribed by the hieratic code. Behind these nations, the cats, ibixes, and crocodiles contemporary with them—rendered monstrous of aspect by their swathing bands—mewed, flapped their wings, or extended their jaws in a saurian giggle.

All the Pharaohs were there—Cheops, Chephrenes, Psammetichus, Sesostris, Amenotaph—all the dark rulers of the pyramids and syrinxes. On yet higher thrones sat Chronos and Xixouthros, who was contemporary with the deluge, and Tubal Cain, who reigned before it.

The beard of King Xixouthros had grown seven times around the granite table upon which he leaned, lost in deep reverie, and buried in dreams.

Further back, through a dusty cloud, I beheld dimly the seventy-two pre-adamite kings, with their seventy-two peoples, for ever passed away.

After permitting me to gaze upon this bewildering spectacle a few moments, the Princess Hermonthis presented me to her father Pharaoh, who favoured me with a most gracious nod.

'I have found my foot again! I have found my foot!' cried the princess, clapping her little hands together with every sign of frantic joy. 'It was this gentleman who restored it to me.'

The races of Kemi, the races of Nahasi—all the black, bronzed, and copper-coloured nations repeated in chorus:

'The Princess Hermonthis has found her foot again!'

Even Xixouthros himself was visibly affected.

He raised his heavy eyelids, stroked his moustache with his fingers, and turned upon me a glance weighty with centuries.

'By Oms, the dog of Hell, and Tmei, daughter of the Sun and of Truth, this is a brave and worthy lad!' exclaimed Pharaoh, pointing to me with his sceptre, which was terminated with a lotus-flower.

'What recompense do you desire?'

Filled with that daring inspired by dreams in which nothing seems impossible, I asked him for the hand of the Princess Hermonthis. The hand seemed to me a very proper antithetic recompense for the foot.

Pharaoh opened wide his great eyes of glass in astonishment at my witty request.

'What country do you come from, and what is your age?'

'I am a Frenchman, and I am twenty-seven years old venerable Pharaoh.'

'Twenty-seven years old, and he wishes to espouse the Princess Hermonthis who is thirty centuries old!' cried out at once all the Thrones and all the Circles of Nations.

Only Hermonthis herself did not seem to think my request unreasonable.

'If you were even only two thousand years old,' replied the ancient king, 'I would willingly give you the princess, but the disproportion is too great; and, besides, we must give our daughters husbands who will last well. You do not know how to preserve yourselves any longer. Even those who died only fifteen centuries ago are already no more than a handful of dust. Behold, my flesh is solid as basalt, my bones are bars of steel!

'I will be present on the last day of the world with the same body and the same features which I had during my lifetime. My daughter Hermonthis will last longer than a statue of bronze.

'Then the last particles of your dust will have been scattered abroad by the winds, and even Isis herself, who was able to find the atoms of Osiris, would scarce be able to recompose your being.

'See how vigorous I yet remain, and how mighty is my grasp,' he added, shaking my hand in the English fashion with a strength that buried my rings in the flesh of my fingers.

He squeezed me so hard that I awoke, and found my friend Alfred shaking me by the arm to make me get up.

'Oh, you everlasting sleeper! Must I have you carried out into the middle of the street, and fireworks exploded in your ears? It is afternoon. Don't you recollect your promise to take me with you to see M. Aguado's Spanish pictures?'

'God! I forgot all, all about it,' I answered, dressing myself hurriedly. 'We will go there at once. I have the permit lying there on my desk.'

I started to find it, but fancy my astonishment when I beheld, instead of the mummy's foot I had purchased the evening before, the little green paste idol left in its place by the Princess Hermonthis!